KILLING

THE AMERICAN DREAM

KILLING
THE AMERICAN DREAM

HOW ANTI-IMMIGRATION EXTREMISTS ARE DESTROYING THE NATION

PILAR MARRERO

palgrave
macmillan

KILLING THE AMERICAN DREAM
Copyright © C. A. Press, 2012.
English-language translation copyright © 2012 by Pilar Marrero
All rights reserved.

First published in the United States as *El Despertar del Sueño Americano*
by C. A. Press

First published in English in 2012 by PALGRAVE MACMILLAN® in the
US—a division of St. Martin's Press LLC, 175 Fifth Avenue, New York,
NY 10010.

Where this book is distributed in the UK, Europe and the rest of the
world, this is by Palgrave Macmillan, a division of Macmillan Publishers
Limited, registered in England, company number 785998, of Houndmills,
Basingstoke, Hampshire RG21 6XS.

Palgrave Macmillan is the global academic imprint of the above
companies and has companies and representatives throughout the world.

Palgrave® and Macmillan® are registered trademarks in the United
States, the United Kingdom, Europe and other countries.

ISBN 978-0-230-34175-3

Library of Congress Cataloging-in-Publication Data

Marrero, Pilar.
   Killing the American dream : how anti-immigration extremists are
destroying the nation / by Pilar Marrero.
      pages   cm
   ISBN 978-0-230-34175-3 (hardback)
      1. United States—Emigration and immigration—Government policy.
2. Illegal aliens—Government policy—United States. 3. Immigrants—
Government policy—United States. 4. Illegal aliens—United States—
Social conditions. 5. Immigrants—United States—Social conditions.
6. Latin Americans—United States—Social conditions. I. Title.
JV6483.M2995   2012
325.73—dc23

                                                            2012014155

A catalogue record of the book is available from the British Library.

Design by Letra Libre, Inc.

First edition: October 2012

10 9 8 7 6 5 4 3 2 1

Printed in the United States of America.

CONTENTS

FOREWORD

ROBERT GUEST

Business Editor of The Economist *and author of* Borderless Economics: Chinese Sea Turtles, Indian Fridges and the New Fruits of Global Capitalism

MY THREE CHILDREN ARE DEVOTED TO "HORRIBLE HISTORIES." IT'S A WONDER-ful romp of a television program that depicts the past in all its smelly, bloody awfulness. It shows, for example, Aztec priests boasting about ripping out the hearts of sacrificial victims, and Saxons giving each other presents of dung (a useful gift in the days before chemical fertilizers).

One sketch depicts the Luddites singing about smashing machines. "Who were the Luddites?" asked Luke, my six-year-old. I explained that they were workers who objected to new technology. During the Industrial Revolution of the nineteenth century, I said, inventors created machines that could weave cotton much faster than a human could do it by hand. That threatened the jobs of weavers, some of whom went around smashing the machines.

I asked Luke whether he thought that was a good idea. Can you halt progress by destroying new inventions? Luke paused for a moment, doubtless to imagine how much fun it would it would be to smash a machine with a hammer, and replied: "No. That's silly."

We then had a chat about the pros and cons of technological change. On the one hand, weaving machines might put weavers out of work. On the other, they produced lots of cheap clothes, so that even poor people could keep warm in winter.

Most people, like my six-year-old, intuitively grasp that the benefits of new technology usually outweigh the costs. For example, machines have destroyed nearly all the jobs in farming, but this is a cause for celebration. In 1800, 75 percent of Americans worked on farms. Now hardly anyone does, because a handful of men on tractors can produce more than enough food to feed everyone else.

Americans are, by and large, technophiles.[1] Yet they are far warier of the other force that makes their country so dynamic: immigration. And that is why Pilar Marrero's new book, *Killing the American Dream,* is so important.

Like new technology, immigration can be disruptive. When foreigners come to America, they bring change. They play new types of music, sometimes loudly. They cook unfamiliar foods, the smells of which waft into other people's backyards. They bring alien customs, some of which native-born Americans may find disconcerting—think of the *hijab* that many Muslim women wear to cover their heads. And they compete with Americans for jobs.

If you like America the way it is, this may trouble you. If you think of the economy in static terms, it may trouble you even more. If there are a fixed number of jobs, and a foreigner takes one, that's one job less for a native-born American, right?

Actually, no. The number of jobs is not fixed. If it was, then the destruction of nearly all agricultural jobs by machines would have left most Americans unemployed. Yet nothing of the sort occurred. On the contrary, the fact that a single combine harvester can cut more corn than dozens of people means that dozens of people are now free to do more rewarding work than wielding a scythe. And more efficient farming makes everyone who eats food better off. A century ago, Americans still devoted 50 percent of their income to putting food on the table. By the turn of the century, that figure had fallen to 10 percent.[2] That's a staggering illustration of progress.

The arrival of new people in America does not have exactly the same effect as the spread of new technology, but there is more overlap than you might think. Like technology, immigration shakes up the comfortable old ways of doing things, but on balance it makes Americans better off.

Immigrants benefit America—and other countries that welcome them—in several ways. First, they bring youth and energy. While other rich countries age and stagnate, America, thanks to a steady influx of immigrants, will remain relatively young for the foreseeable future. The financial crisis ravaging Europe in 2012 is rooted in the fact that there are too few young workers to pay the pensions of legions of retirees. America can avoid this fate—and save Social Security—if it keeps its doors open.

Second, immigrants bring brains. They are some 12 percent of the US population, but account for 26 percent of its Nobel Prize winners and 24 percent of its patent applicants.[3] Immigrants put fizz into American science and technology. They perform 25 percent of the science and engineering jobs, and nearly 40 percent of the jobs in those fields that require PhDs. One study found that every immigrant with an advanced degree in science or technology from an American university creates on average 2.6 new American jobs.[4]

Third, immigrants bring a spirit of enterprise. Leaving your home country to strike out into the unknown requires get up and go. So migrants are often exceptional people. Silicon Valley would be lost without them: nearly half of the top fifty venture-capital backed firms in the United States have at least one immigrant founder.[5] In New York, immigrants are 36 percent of the population but half of all small-business owners. In some fields, they are even more prominent: they run 70 to 90 percent of New York's taxi firms, grocery stores, day care centers, and laundry businesses. Overall in America, newcomers are twice as likely as the native-born to start a new company.

These three benefits of immigration—youth, brains, and enterprise—are reasonably familiar, albeit underappreciated. But there are also two less obvious benefits. The first is that migrants bring a fresh perspective. People who come from elsewhere often look at their new home and see things that are invisible to locals. The second is that migrants bring connections. They know people back home, and form bridges between America and the rest of the world.

Both of these non-obvious benefits are illustrated by the story of Cheung Yan, a Chinese businesswoman. When she moved from China to America in the early 1990s, she made two observations. The first was that Americans throw away mountains of waste paper—junk mail, election pamphlets, old catalogues, and so forth. The second was that container ships sail from China to America fully laden, but return half-empty.

This is because the things China exports to America take up a lot of space: televisions, steel girders, this year's must-have plastic toys and so forth. But the things America sends back are often weightless: Hollywood movies, intellectual property, and IOUs from the government.

Cheung Yan turned these two insights into a multi-billion dollar business. She gathered up American waste paper and sent it to China on those half-empty ships. She used her contacts in China to set up factories to recycle waste paper into cardboard. (This point is important. In emerging markets where the rule of law is patchy, you need to know people to do business. Otherwise you are likely to be ripped off, and the courts cannot be relied upon to help you.)

Much of that recycled cardboard was then used to make boxes, many of which were no doubt packed with televisions and sent back to America. Cheung Yan is now a billionaire. Her business, Nine Dragons Paper, is typical of the businesses that migrants start: it is neither simply American nor simply Chinese, but a fertile mixture of the two.

The world is full of budding Cheung Yans. In my travels as *The Economist* magazine's business editor, I meet them all the time.

America would be wise to welcome such people; but often it does not. Ms. Marrero gives a good example in Chapter 9. In the fall of 2011, Detlev Hager, a top executive from Mercedes-Benz was driving through Alabama. He was pulled over by police, who demanded to see his papers. Unfortunately for Hager, he did not have his driver's license with him. Nor did he have his German passport, though he did have a German identity document.

He was arrested. A draconian new law in Alabama, taking its cue from a similar law in Arizona, requires the police to check the immigration status of anyone they suspect of being in the country illegally. The aim of the law is to make life so unpleasant for undocumented immigrants that they deport themselves, saving America the expense of rounding them up and putting them on buses with barred windows.

Lawmakers should be careful what they wish for, however. Forcing the police to devote valuable thief-catching time to harassing foreigners will discourage foreign investment. Mercedes-Benz has created thousands of jobs in Alabama, both at its factory in Tuscaloosa and at the companies that supply it with car parts. Those jobs may not be immediately at risk—it is not easy to move a factory that has already been built. But if the Yellowhammer State earns a reputation for xenophobia, future foreign investors may shun it.

Other states are eager to woo them. As Ms. Marrero describes, a few days after the German executive was arrested, the *St. Louis Post-Dispatch* in Missouri ran an op-ed piece titled "Hey,

Mercedes, Time to Move to a More Welcoming State." "We are the 'Show Me' state, not the 'show me your papers' state," the article said.

Ms. Marrero is one of the most compassionate voices in America's immigration debate. She knows the subject well because she has reported on it for so long: she worked for *La Opinión,* a leading Spanish-language newspaper, for 19 years and is now a syndicated columnist. And she understands the subject at a visceral level because she has lived it.

She was born in Venezuela and moved to America in 1986, pulled by the usual forces. She was tempted by the adventure of living abroad. She wanted to "live in the First World, where public services actually worked and the streets were safer." And she wanted to be with her boyfriend (who later became her husband), a Venezuelan who had already upped sticks to Los Angeles.

America is the only important nation founded on an idea. Most other countries are built on the fact that a particular tribe occupies a particular piece of land. America is built on the idea that "all men are created equal" and have an "unalienable right" to "the pursuit of happiness." Those words from the Declaration of Independence undergird the American Dream: the idea that if you come to America, work hard, and play by the rules, you can build a good life.

Having chased this dream and caught it, Ms. Marrero is clearly upset to see so many of her compatriots abandon it. Personally, I think she is a bit too pessimistic when she says that anti-immigration extremists are "destroying the nation," but they are certainly hacking at its foundations with a pickax.

A flashback to the 1980s in Ms. Marrero's first chapter shows how much less generous the rhetoric has become. The Berlin Wall was not the only barrier Ronald Reagan found objectionable. "Rather than talking about putting up a fence [between the United States and Mexico], why don't we work out recognition of our mutual problems, [and] make it possible to come legally with a work permit?" he said at a Republican debate in 1980. His opponent, George H. W. Bush, agreed: "These are good people, strong people . . . part of my family is Mexican."

By the 1990s, the political atmosphere was growing pricklier. Ms. Marrero describes the furious tussle over California's Proposition 187 in 1994, a ballot initiative that barred the state from providing most social services (including education) to illegal immigrants. The measure was eventually ruled unconstitutional, but its immigrant-scapegoating spirit has spread. Jack Kemp, who was later a Republican vice-presidential nominee, said it "corrodes the soul" of the Republican Party.

In the 2000s, George W. Bush made a serious effort to enact a pragmatic immigration reform. He pushed for a visa system that reflected the nation's economic needs, and a path to legalization for undocumented migrants who worked, paid taxes, and broke no other laws. He was backed by immigrant-friendly lawmakers from both parties, principally John McCain of Arizona and the late Ted Kennedy of Massachusetts. But restrictionists from both parties scuppered his efforts at reform. Some Republicans banged a nativist drum, pandering to voters who simply dislike foreigners. Some Democrats were lukewarm about reform, too, mindful that many of their blue-collar supporters fear that immigrants will take their jobs. A good bill died.

Since then, the federal government has failed miserably to address America's broken immigration system. When campaigning for president in 2008, Barack Obama promised a reform very similar to George Bush's proposal. He told a Spanish-language television network: "I can guarantee that during the first year of my term, we will have an immigration reform package [in Congress] which I will vigorously support, and will personally promote. And I want to do this as quickly as possible." He broke that promise.

Ms. Marrero's disappointment with Mr. Obama—the son of an immigrant—is palpable. He made no serious effort to pass immigration reform during his first term. Instead, he enforced the old laws ruthlessly. In Chapter 13, Ms. Marrero describes "The Perfection of the Deportation Machine." More than a million undocumented migrants were arrested and deported from America in the first three years of Mr. Obama's presidency. "The actions of his administration have been diametrically opposed to the content of his speeches," sighs Ms. Marrero. (Her book was written before Mr. Obama announced, in June 2012, that he would stop deporting quite so many people. But even this welcome change fell far short of what the candidate Obama promised.)

America's recent souring on immigration is perhaps unsurprising. Nations undergoing severe economic trauma—as America has since the collapse of Lehman Brothers in 2008—often turn inward. But it is nonetheless un-American. The country was founded on mass immigration and would be a backwater without it.

No one expects America, or any other country, to have completely open borders any time soon. But it is essential to keep the door ajar, to allow people with talent and youth and drive to spend time on American soil. Some will stay and settle. Others will study and work for a few years and then go home. Either way, America benefits.

In my view, the world has entered a new age of migration. Not only are there more first-generation migrants than ever before: more than 215 million, or 3 percent of the global population. They are also better connected.

It used to be that a migrant would hop on a boat, sail to America and promptly lose touch with the country he came from. No more. These days a typical newcomer will text his mother as soon as the plane hits the runway. He can follow the news from his home town via the Internet, stay in touch with his old classmates via social media and send money home in minutes.

Easy communication allow migrants to remain constantly and intimately in touch with the places they came from. That means they create networks, which speed the flow of trade, information and ideas across borders. A nation that can plug into these networks will be richer and more creative, just as a laptop connected to the Internet is far more powerful than one that stands alone.[6]

America, as the nation with the largest population of immigrants, is the best-placed to plug into the vast global web of interconnection that migrants create. This is a good reason to bet on America remaining the world's indispensable power, despite the rise of China.

It ought to be easy to persuade a nation built by immigrants to keep the door ajar. But it isn't. The nativists have the best sound-bites, and some deep human instincts supporting their cause. Those who favor openness must make their case clearly, consistently and concretely. Few people are moved by studies showing the economic benefits of migration. But many can relate to stories of flesh-and-blood human beings who migrate to find a better life.

Ms. Marrero tells these stories with passion and conviction. *Killing the American Dream* is, oddly enough, a step towards saving it.

London, June 2012

INTRODUCTION

WHEN I STARTED WORKING IN LOS ANGELES IN 1987, ONE OF MY FIRST ASSIGN-
ments as a new reporter was covering the implementation of the
Immigration and Control Act of 1986, which allowed millions of
undocumented immigrants to achieve their dream of legal residency in the United States.

I remember some colorful events verging on the ridicu-
lous. For example, two local directors of the Immigration and
Naturalization Service, the regional director, Harold Ezell, and
the head of the Los Angeles INS office, Ernest Gustafson, went
around the city wearing big sombreros, along with popular local
disc jockey Luis Roberto "El Tigre" Gonzalez, urging undocumented immigrants to take advantage of the program.

They were dubbed "el Trio *Amnistía,*" or the Amnesty Trio.

What a different time that was, when the word "amnesty"
meant just what the dictionary says: a general pardon for offenses,
particularly political offenses. In this legislation, the US government pardoned those present in the country illegally and granted
official permanent residency, under certain conditions.

Today, amnesty is a profoundly controversial issue in the
United States. The term itself has become almost a dirty word,

spat contemptuously when talking about the "illegals," the label used to describe unauthorized immigrants in the country. The way in which the use of the word "amnesty" and what it implies has changed reflects something deeper: the sea change in attitude toward certain immigrants that has swept the United States over the past twenty-five years.

For me, as a relatively recently arrived Latin American immigrant at the time, the Amnesty Trio was a surprising phenomenon, underscoring how important Mexican, Central American, and other Latino immigrants were to modern life and US power as a whole. Perhaps since I was Venezuelan instead of Mexican, I did not have a clear concept of the importance of recent immigrants to the United States. It wasn't something that was taught in school, and it wasn't covered in any of the world history classes I took.

When I was born in the mid-1960s, the United States was the world's number one economic superpower, and it still was when I immigrated to Los Angeles in 1986, following my Venezuelan boyfriend who later became my husband. Even though I grew up in a working-class family, unlike millions of others who went north, my motivations for immigrating were not economic: I could have stayed in Venezuela and pursued my career as a journalist there after graduating from Andres Bello Catholic University in Caracas in 1986.

But in addition to my relationship with my partner, who had lived in the United States for years, I was attracted to the idea of going abroad. I wanted to see other countries and live in the First World, where public services actually worked and the streets were safer. Many Latin Americans can understand this: We love our countries, but we wish they were different. Sometimes the only realistic option that occurs to us is to leave and go off in search of brighter horizons.

So besides following my romantic relationship, I emigrated in search of my very own American Dream, a dream that is not necessarily the same for everyone: to leave my country, gain independence from my family, and experience life in a "developed" country.

When I arrived in Los Angeles, it quickly became clear that the reality was much more complex than the vision I had had in my head. The impressions I had of America came from television shows and movies, where you rarely ever saw an actor of color, and what life was really like for minorities and immigrants in the major cities, much less small towns, was never portrayed.

To me, the United States was the egalitarian society of *Star Trek,* personified by the handsome Captain Kirk, or the idealized suburban lifestyle of Samantha Stevens the pretty blond witch on *Bewitched.* The only Latino we saw was, of course, *I Love Lucy's* Ricky Ricardo, whose accent didn't seem strange to us at all, since everything was dubbed into Spanish anyway.

In the 1980s, Los Angeles was a boiling pot of immigrants, refugees from the wars in Central America, and gangs, mostly African American but also Latino, and killings happened every day. In the first few years after moving to Los Angeles, I experienced and covered events as serious as a spate of highway shootings that completely terrified this metropolis that was so dependent on the car; abuse within the city's police department; the Rodney King case and the trials of the police officers involved who had delivered over fifty blows to the African American motorist; and, later, the 1992 riots that followed the officers' acquittal of excessive force charges. These were tumultuous, troubled years in the life of Los Angeles and they would serve as a basis for reforms that would lead to a more modern, progressive city.

In this nation that was much more complicated than the myth, Latin Americans played an increasingly important role as workers, neighbors, residents, and citizens. As a result of the Central American wars, the Amnesty Law of 1986, and the strong economy of the 1990s, this country saw the biggest influx of immigrants in modern times. The robust workforce rejuvenated the population and also created social pressures in major cities and smaller cities and towns.

Still, being undocumented in those years was not as trying as it would become after 1996 and especially after 2001. But because of opportunistic politicians who opted for legislating immigration law in fragments, immigration law became a complicated nightmare: only the next election mattered to them, not the long-term needs of the country and its economy.

For decades, it was possible to live peacefully undocumented: People could work and get state identity cards and driver's licenses. The border—the back door—was ajar, and the laws allowed for those with a family or employer sponsors greater possibilities to become legal.

The Amnesty Law legalized and integrated 3 million people into American society, but it failed to create long-term mechanisms for hiring foreign workers in the industries that would most need them according to fluctuations in the economy. Also, up through the mid-1990s, border control measures were not enforced adequately, nor was it possible to contain the proliferation of false documents because of the staunch opposition to creating a national identity card. That opposition continues today, but the enforcement mechanisms available through the sharing of fingerprints and other personal information among federal and state authorities have vastly improved enforcement with time. Still, 11 million unauthorized immigrants still live, work, and often prosper in the United States, providing key sectors of the economy with a flexible, young, and energetic labor force.

The reality is that the United States has always been, is, and will most likely continue to be a magnet for desperate or ambitious immigrants. As long as there is no simple, effective immigration system with sufficient numbers of work visas in place, no amnesty, no matter how broad, and no border wall will block the future flow of "illegal" immigrants if the country continues to hold out its most precious treasure: a job, and the chance to succeed.

Since the years of the Amnesty Trio in the mid-1980s, California governor Pete Wilson's electoral maneuverings in 1994, and radical changes in immigration law in 1996, the lives of undocumented immigrants and their loved ones who are legal residents and citizens have become infinitely more difficult. The United States has not had the will to carry out massive deportations of millions of undocumented people or to sincerely consider the crucial role they play in the nation's economy. We continue, as a country, to live in an increasingly uncomfortable state of limbo. This situation is no longer sustainable politically. Because the issue remains unresolved at a time when the global power of the United States is in a state of decline, it also is no longer sustainable economically or morally.

Radical islamic terrorism and the rise of China and India as global competitors for superpower status now threaten the United States's number-one status. This is not the first time in history that immigrants have been used as cannon fodder on the political battlefield—held responsible for problems and failings of the country—rather than being seen as an integral part of who we Americans are and who we have always been.

And so at this point of the twenty-first century, the United States is a country that idealizes its immigrant origins but cannot understand the importance of its present-day immigrants. For the first time in recent history, the United States of America is becoming a country that is hostile to the newly arrived. Laws and immigration politics are controlled by extremist minorities who manipulate public opinion and who have successfully blocked the passage of measures meant to integrate these newest Americans. The fact that the most recent arrivals are only slightly or in no way different from their own immigrant ancestors is something the extremists conveniently leave out of the conversation.

Critics point out that the problem is in the "illegality" of these immigrants, asking "What part of 'illegal' don't you understand?" A virtual industry of candidates and political functionaries has sustained itself on this concept, yet none has done much to actually formulate long-term solutions to the problem. The fact is, the same things were said about the destitute, desperate immigrants who arrived from Europe on ships. They were not illegal only because there were no legal restrictions in place, but they were considered just as threatening. Yet they were still let in, were employed, and became integrated into the fabric of this great society.

The current situation is not without peril. The negative tone and the restrictive measures being adopted against immigrants threaten the social and economic stability of a country that achieved greatness because of the foreigners who came here across the centuries to work in the hardest, most critical jobs, enabling those who came before them to progress even more.

Demographic and economic experts are sounding the alarm.

Dowell Myers, professor at the School of Policy, Planning and Development at the University of Southern California, explains why immigrants are crucial for the country, especially within the context of an aging population. "This tsunami of aging threatens to flood our economy with too many retirees and home sellers and overwhelm our government with the needs of aged dependents. The aging crisis is a true emergency and the children of immigrants have a crucial role to play," Myers asserts.[1]

Nevertheless, this future necessity for a young, diverse, and productive labor force seems to have no effect on immigration politics. Immigration reform has become an untouchable topic, and the advocates for more and more restrictions keep winning every battle, even when it goes against the national interest.

This lack of will for reform was reflected, for example, in the defeat of the Development, Relief, and Education for Alien Minors (DREAM) Act in Congress in December 2010. The measure would have granted legal status to qualified young undocumented immigrants attending college or serving in the military who were brought to this country as children by their parents—true Americans in terms of culture and upbringing. This extraordinary generation is confronting crippling limitations that previous generations of immigrants never had to face.[2]

And consider the state laws passed in Alabama, Arizona, and Georgia that allow—or, perhaps more accurately, *require*—local police to demand papers from people who might be undocumented. It permits any ordinary citizen to sue a police officer for failing to enforce the law and criminalizes the mere act of seeking work or hiring someone off any street corner, a precedent that goes further than any other in this country's legal history. Each of these states has felt the negative economic consequences of the restrictive measures, an effect that threatens to be long lasting, although the courts considering challenges to the laws will have the last word.[3]

The political class pushing for ever-more restrictive measures cannot be bothered to consider that these laws could have disastrous economic and societal effects. The blame for this lack of vision largely rests with certain politicians who exploit voters' fears regarding security and the lingering recession for their own personal gain. For almost two decades, politicians have used the worst stereotypes to describe foreigners in general, and especially Mexicans, transforming them into convenient symbols for everything that "threatens" the country.

This purposeful stoking of our basest fears has helped give rise to an increasing number of hate groups in regions of the country, groups setting their sights not on blacks or Jews, as in days past, but on "illegals" (read: brown-skinned Latin Americans).

According to the Southern Poverty Law Center, the number of radical groups that carry out direct actions to confront and harass immigrants is growing at an alarming rate. For example, just between 2008 and 2009, the number of hate groups grew from 173 to 309, an increase of 80 percent. Consider the Minuteman Project, which popped up in different areas across the country not simply to protest against immigrants but to actively report them, harass them, and guard the border with Mexico, vigilante style, to catch undocumented immigrants attempting to cross.

The consequences of these phenomena are clearly apparent. An editorial in the *New York Times* published in December 2010 raised a warning. Titled "Immigration Hardball," the piece anticipated that over the course of the next two years, radicals in Congress would not try to come up with real solutions to the issue of unauthorized immigration but would instead continue to emphasize more of the same: enforcement solutions. "That hard-line approach mocks American values. It is irresponsibly expensive. It is ineffective."[4] In other words, there is a price to pay.

Predictably, some Republicans in Congress announced plans to reevaluate the constitutional right to citizenship for all children born on American soil. Although some European countries have taken away what in the US Constitution is a fundamental right of birth granting citizenship, not only has the action failed to solve their own immigration problems, but it also has given rise to more problems by creating a permanent underclass of residents with no country to call their own and no future.

The growing hostility to immigrants goes against our country's vibrant history and raises troubling moral questions. In recent years, the increasingly aggressive and accelerated deportation of undocumented immigrants has torn families apart and fostered a permanent population of second-class people. Most people are unaware of the danger this poses for the nation's long-term survival: The world's sole superpower, increasingly competing with the growing economies of China and India, cannot maintain current levels of prosperity without fully integrating the millions of immigrants who are already here into society.

By being denied access to the "American Dream"—to achieve a comfortable middle-class existence, the goal of all recent arrivals—immigrants will not be the only ones adversely affected: All Americans will lose out, experiencing negative effects on the economy and the country as a whole.

The lack of progress on this population's status leads to an obvious outcome: When immigrants cannot legitimize their presence and move up the social ladder to join the ranks of the middle class and achieve the American Dream, the broader society cannot make full use of the engine of economic and social energy that immigrants could provide by revitalizing declining neighborhoods; helping others up the economic ladder; and allowing aging baby boomers to retire, receive their pensions and social security, and sell their homes.

It is painful to see how little lawmakers have learned from the past. In early 2012, as the dwindling field of Republican hopefuls vied for their party's nomination for the presidency, some mentioned making English the "official language of the government"—an entirely unnecessary measure, since English is already the de facto official language of the government and the country. One candidate's short-lived defense of letting undocumented students attend college was somehow viewed as highly controversial.

Meanwhile, other candidates believed all immigrants should "go back home and get in line with everybody else" and then immigrate legally while they failed to present any ideas on how to change existing laws in order to make that scenario remotely feasible.[5] Current law would make it impossible for most of them to reenter the country for several years. They would have to leave lives and family behind, wreaking havoc on communities. There's no real scenario for the orderly regularization of this population, barring major reforms of the immigration laws of this country.

That concept, advocated by the Republican nominee, former Massachusetts governor Mitt Romney, assumes that there is no reason for the United States to consider how the country may benefit from the presence of millions of immigrants who have worked, lived, paid taxes, and raised families in this country, as all the past waves of immigrants have done before them.

Romney's own family emigrated, when his great-grandfather Miles Park Romney fled across the border to Mexico in the 1800s to escape the anti-polygamist laws of his own country and live freely in Mexico, where there were no laws on the books prohibiting polygamy, and in spite of it being a very Catholic country, Mormons could live—at least in their colony—without fear of prosecution, unlike in the United States.

Politicians sound off about eliminating the magnet that attracts undocumented immigrants. But it is clear that the day that magnet is gone, and immigrants along with it, it will be the beginning of the end of the United States of America.

PART I
TWENTY-FIVE YEARS OF IMMIGRATION POLITICS
FROM RONALD REAGAN'S AMNESTY TO THE PERSECUTION OF "ILLEGALS"

ONE
"I BELIEVE IN AMNESTY"
RONALD REAGAN, THE 1986 LAW, AND UNFINISHED REFORM

RONALD REAGAN IS WIDELY VIEWED AS THE PATRON SAINT OF THE REPUBLICAN Party. Republicans idolize Reagan, president of the United States from 1980 to 1988, as their quintessential leader and the most important president of modern times. Every four years, Republican candidates hoping to win their party's nomination and move into the White House make a sacred pilgrimage to Simi Valley, an upper-class white suburban enclave about 50 miles outside of Los Angeles, and hold a debate at the Ronald Reagan Presidential Foundation and Library, in the shadow of the very Air Force One that once ferried the president around the world.

The Reagan library houses the life and work of the president who always had a jar full of jelly beans on his desk and who had a successful career as a Hollywood actor and president of the Screen Actors' Guild before turning his attentions to conservative politics. Most of Reagan's transformation to what he is now, the ultimate icon of conservatism and independence, took place after his death in 2004.

Beyond everything else that Reagan stands for and the many controversies his administration became mired in—especially the Iran–Contra scandal and the US government support for paramilitary groups in Nicaragua, El Salvador, and Guatemala—the former president is fondly remembered with great nostalgia by traditional conservatives, who consider him a true champion of their cause.

But there is one issue that Reagan's loyal admirers prefer to gloss over or to imagine that, if he were alive today, he would think and act on very differently than he did in the 1980s: Reagan's position on undocumented immigration. Even though a political current at that time advocated for hard-line measures against undocumented immigrants, the tone and scope of the discussion was very different from what is occurring today.

For those of us who have grown accustomed to the sharp, hostile tone in which the immigration debate has been cast over the past fifteen years, it is surprising and even refreshing to watch an exchange on undocumented immigration between Ronald Reagan and George H. W. Bush at a 1980 primary Republican debate, which we can do thanks to the magic of YouTube.[1]

At that event, a young man in the audience asks both candidates if they believe that children of unauthorized immigrants should receive a free public education. To today's viewers, the answers of both presidential contenders are nothing short of shocking. One wishes that these two conservative leaders of the 1980s could counsel their party's current leadership on the issue.

Bush answered, "I'd like to see something done about the illegal alien problem that would be so sensitive and understanding of the labor needs and human needs that this problem would not come up. If those people are here, I would reluctantly say they would get what society is giving to their neighbors."

What Bush says next goes right to the heart of the matter. His observation is completely consistent with what analysts and historians who study immigration agree on but is something that would never come out of a leading politician's mouth today. And that includes most Democrats, the party that supposedly favors immigrants.

Said Bush: "But the problem is we are making *illegal* the labor that I'd like to see legal. We are doing two things, we are creating a whole society of really honorable, decent family loving people that are in violation of the law and second . . . we exacerbate relations with Mexico."

Bush added, "The answer is more fundamental than whether they attend Houston schools. If they're here, I don't want to see a bunch of six-, eight-year-old kids that are totally uneducated and made to feel that they're living outside the law, let's address the fundamentals . . . these are *good* people, *strong* people . . . part of my family is Mexican!" Bush expressed himself with all of the heartfelt passion that his reserved character would permit.

Then it was the turn of Reagan, who went on to win the Republican nomination and the presidential election that year. "I think the time has come that the US and Mexico have a better relationship than we've ever had. We haven't been sensitive enough with our power. They have forty to fifty percent unemployment . . . this cannot continue without possibility of trouble below the border . . . and we could have a very hostile and estranged neighbor on our border," said Reagan, who feared that the influence of Cuba and Mexico's poverty could be an explosive mix that would unleash a revolution.

"Rather than talking about putting up a fence, why don't we work out recognition of our mutual problems, make it possible to come legally with a work permit, while working they pay taxes . . . they can go back, cross the border both ways," Reagan said.

Did this debate really happen? Did the candidates really say that? It's not some kind of YouTube hoax? It's simply amazing that Reagan was categorically opposed to a border fence and that both Republican candidates offered thoughtful answers and believed that the problem had to be solved rationally. Shrill warnings of illegals pouring over the border and taking over the country had not yet come to dominate the immigration discussion within the Republican Party, as they would in the 1990s and beyond.

Reagan talked about the critical importance of maintaining good relations with Mexico and having a system that would allow the free flow of labor: practically an open border, with some regulation. Reagan was more concerned with his southern neighbor's vulnerability to a guerrilla movement like the Castro regime that had prevailed in Cuba or the Sandinistas, then gaining strength in Nicaragua, than the effects immigrants were having on the United States. He understood that immigrant labor was necessary and that the presence of such workers could be regulated.

In a 1979 diary entry, Reagan wrote about a private meeting he was going to have with Mexican president José López Portillo: He hoped they would "discuss how the United States and Mexico could make the border 'something other than the location for a fence.'"[2]

The leader who years later would utter the famous phrase demanding the demolition of the Berlin Wall and the fall of communism—"Mr. Gorbachev, tear down this wall"—did not want to build a wall along Mexico's border, even when he had made comments on several occasions about unauthorized immigration being a serious problem.

Alan Simpson, the Republican senator from Wyoming who cosponsored the immigration bill of 1986 and who was a close friend of Reagan's, said in an interview in 2010 that the president "knew that it was not right for people to be abused. Anybody who's here illegally is going to be abused in some way, either financially or physically. They have no rights."[3]

Former Reagan speechwriter Peter Robinson said that "it was in Ronald Reagan's bones—it was part of his understanding of America—that the country was fundamentally open to those who wanted to join us here."[4]

As president, Reagan did more than just talk about trying to change the immigration system. In 1986, he signed into law the

Immigration and Control Act (IRCA), which had been passed with bipartisan support in Congress. This legislation would also be known as the Simpson-Mazzoli Law, named after the two senators who sponsored it, Simpson and Roman Mazzoli, a Democratic congressman from Kentucky. It was known more widely as the Amnesty Law. Three million undocumented people were legalized thanks to this legislation.

In a 1984 debate with Democratic presidential candidate Walter Mondale, Reagan said he felt particular contempt for businesses that hired undocumented workers and paid them a substandard wage, knowing they would never complain for fear of being discovered working illegally.[5] These same business interests have, for decades, blocked efforts to create a system that penalizes employers for hiring undocumented workers.

Until that time, no business had ever been sanctioned for that reason in the entire history of the United States. Until 1986, no legal mechanism had even existed for punishing those who provided the biggest single incentive for immigrants to come to this country: jobs.

The first efforts to develop a system for sanctioning employers surfaced in the 1950s. Paul Douglas, a democratic senator from Illinois, proposed imposing formal penalties, but he did not get far with his idea. In 1972, Congressman Peter Rodino, a Democrat representing New Jersey, tried to introduce legislation but that attempt also went nowhere. In 1977, the Democratic Carter administration proposed a law that would impose sanctions on employers. The initiative was quickly shot down by Senator James Eastland, Democrat from Mississippi, a strong advocate for the agriculture industry, which had always vociferously opposed any limitations on its ability to hire cheap labor. Eastland was the Judiciary Committee chair and refused even to hold hearings on it.

But the flow of unauthorized immigrants remained constant, especially after the Bracero Program came to a formal end in

1965. For twenty-five years, the program had allowed hundreds of thousands of Mexican workers to enter the country and work on farms and on the railroads, starting during World War II and continuing for two decades due to ongoing pressure of the agricultural industry, which claimed ongoing labor shortages. As the inflow of illegal immigration increased after the Bracero Program came to an end, in the mid-1970s Edward Kennedy, then a young Democratic senator from Massachusetts, proposed a special commission to study the issue. Those efforts eventually led to the 1986 Immigration Control and Reform Act, IRCA.

The commission's report evaluated all of the existing data available at the time and concluded that immigrants have a generally positive impact on the country because they contribute to economic growth and productivity. The report also issued a serious warning: Undocumented immigration brings a host of problems, and politicians had to do something about it.

Sophia Wallace, a political scientist at the University of Kentucky, emphasizes that in spite of all the goodwill on the part of President Reagan and other politicians, the idea of creating a law to try to solve the illegal immigration problem met with wide resistance from groups on both sides of the political spectrum.

Nonetheless, after several attempts, it was achieved in 1986. IRCA included a series of measures, some of which were implemented more successfully than others: the legalization of undocumented people; heightened border security; sanctions against businesses or employers who hired undocumented workers; funds to assist local governments—states received $4 billion over four years to provide services to newly legalized immigrants; and a legalization program for agricultural workers.

Dolores Huerta, cofounder of the United Farm Workers union, along with farm worker leader Cesar Chavez, pointed out to me in an interview that pressures from Southern congressmen, particularly Republicans, with close ties to the agricultural industry played a key role in Reagan's support of the final version of IRCA.

More than 1 million farm workers gained legal status, and for years the agricultural industry suffered no labor shortages. It was assumed that working conditions would improve as a result of legalization, but in the long run, the agricultural industry continued to keep the cost of labor as low as they possibly could. Eventually, a large number of jobs were filled by subcontractors, who in turn hired undocumented workers.

In all, 3 million undocumented immigrants were granted "amnesty" under IRCA. But critics considered the law a failure because it did not deter the arrival of more undocumented immigrants. The sponsors of the law, Simpson and Mazzoli, later published an article in the *Washington Post* explaining how IRCA had not worked as they had hoped it would: "We believe that the shortcomings of the act are not due to design failure but rather to the failure of both Democratic and Republican administrations since 1986 to execute the law properly," they wrote.[6]

According to their article, the most successful part of IRCA was the legalization of 3 million undocumented people, a population that had been forced to live in the shadows, vulnerable to exploitation, and through the law could become an integral part of the US workforce and society as a whole. Studies also showed that the legalized immigrants benefited financially and socially and were generally no longer subject to exploitation and abuse in the workplace.

But according to Simpson and Mazzoli, the federal government did not begin allocating adequate funds to border control until ten years after the law had passed; that money was sorely needed to manage what had been up until then a very porous border. And groups on both the right and the left were opposed to creating a national identity card, which the law's sponsors had envisioned as a vital element to its success. The idea was that job seekers would have to present this uniform means of identification to potential employers before being hired and in order to obtain benefits.

"After two decades, the system is still not in place. Unfortunately, what is in place is the use of several different identifiers, which were meant to be temporary, and a flourishing underground economy engaged in creating fraudulent documents for illegal immigrants," the article points out.

This was the essential problem in the law's application: The necessary tools were not in place to effectively enforce the sanctions against employers, sanctions that were included in a federal law for the first time in US history. In the world of politics, both the right and the left also attacked this part of the law.

The right criticized sanctions as excessive and intrusive regulation into business activities that constituted exerting artificial controls on the labor market, going against the sacred principles of the free market economy.

The left viewed employer sanctions as discriminatory, because they meant that companies would ask potential employees for documentation based on the color of their skin. Some studies from the late eighties did verify the existence of just this kind of racial profiling.[7]

The libertarian perspective—an integral part of US politics since colonial times, based on the notion that liberty means government should intervene in business as little as possible—rabidly opposed the use of a national identity card, something fairly common in other countries but that has never existed in the United States.

This one uniform identity card would have been preferable, according to Simpson and Mazzoli, to the dozens of forms of identification used to verify the nationality and eligibility of job seekers for work. And the lack of such a card was a key reason that the Amnesty Law did not work.

Before 1986, the closest thing to employer sanctions was the 1952 Immigration and Nationality Act, which said it was illegal to "harbor" undocumented immigrants. But a section called the "Texas Proviso" stated that employment was not considered "harboring," so it was essentially legal for employers to hire undocumented workers, even if their presence in the country was illegal. After 1986, all employers had to do to comply with the law was demonstrate they had filled in the proper forms (the I–9, created by the Immigration and Nationality Act), providing information on each employee.

The results of this approach are not surprising: By maintaining a supply of jobs open to undocumented workers in certain sectors of the economy, illegal immigration continued unabated, especially when the country experienced economic growth. IRCA did not include any kind of mechanism for adapting the laws to the country's economic conditions. Instead, it preserved fixed numerical quotas already in place in various programs for workers.

History has shown that no border fence or number of agents along the border can stop the flow of immigrants as long as a jobs incentive exists and as long as a country with a massive population living in poverty shares a long border with a wealthy one.

But the politicians looking for easy answers, especially ones that would attract voters, keep on telling Americans that illegal immigration is a law enforcement issue, not an economic one. "You have to control the border, and I know just how to do it," most politicians assert, repeating the same tired slogans.

As other similar experiments throughout history have shown, no wall, no matter how tightly controlled it may be (think of the Berlin Wall, which divided the city of Berlin and East and West Germany from 1961 until 1980) can keep out someone who is desperate and determined enough to get past it.

"Build a thirty-foot wall, and you'll see a lot of thirty-one-foot ladders," Bill Richardson, the former governor of New Mexico and a 2008 candidate for the Democratic presidential nomination, often stated. "That wall is never going to work."

In recent years, the US government's approach to curbing illegal immigration has been focused strictly on controlling the border, especially since the mid-1990s. Although these measures of border control are probably necessary, they are not enough to solve the fundamental problem. Something has to be done about the status of 11 million undocumented immigrants living in the country, many of whom are so thoroughly enmeshed in the nation's economic and social fabric that they cannot be removed without causing enormous damage to their communities and without affecting the future needs of the US economy.

IRCA was the last major, bold attempt to address the problem of illegal immigration in a comprehensive way. But it was not successful, because politicians lacked the political will to really turn the screws on employers hiring undocumented workers and to punish them with any meaningful sanctions.

In practice, hiring undocumented workers continues to be more beneficial than costly for both businesses and private citizens looking for household help. That is why illegal immigration has been unstoppable and why it will continue to be unstoppable until that equation changes. Though illegal crossings have slowed to a trickle during the Great Recession that the United States is still experiencing, the magnet is likely to come back in force with the economic recovery and the aging of the US population.

TWO

CALIFORNIA CASTS
THE FIRST STONE

Unless the stream of their importation could be turned . . . they will soon so out number us, that all the advantages we have, will not in my opinion be able to preserve our language, and even our Government will become precarious. Why should Pennsylvania, founded by the English, *become a Colony of Aliens, who will shortly be so numerous as to Germanize us instead of our Anglifying them, and will never adopt our Language or Customs, any more than they can acquire our Complexion.*

— Benjamin Franklin, in a letter on German immigrants

IN LATE 1993, A SMALL GROUP OF PEOPLE GOT TOGETHER IN A MEXICAN REStaurant in Orange, California, and formed an organization that would thereafter be known by its initials, which happened to be the same as the international distress signal: SOS, Save Our State. A few months later, SOS presented a ballot initiative to California's secretary of state, an initiative that would eventually be known as Proposition 187 and would shake national politics to its foundations.

As the founders of SOS came together that day and discussed their goals over Mexican food—no doubt cooked and served by natives of that country—they had no idea how far their initiative would go. In fact, it would become the springboard for many other measures against undocumented immigrants over the next several years and plant the seeds of a profound change in attitudes toward immigrants in general that eventually would sweep the country. At that moment in the last decade of the twentieth century, political circumstances on the state, national, and international levels created the perfect storm for creating a new outlook on immigration.

In the United States, a country formed by European colonizers who arrived in waves over hundreds of years—and who grabbed the land out from under the native population who had been here since prehistoric times—almost every new wave of immigrants and the changes they bring with them has inspired legal efforts to limit, regulate, or exclude them.

Anti-immigrant sentiment has ebbed and flowed over time and, depending on the economic situation, periodically resurfaced with new vigor. This distaste for newcomers has been exploited by politicians and others looking for public recognition. Each new crop of immigrants—Germans, Chinese, Irish, Italians—stirred up resentment among the established society, especially during hard times.

What was going on in the mid-1990s doesn't look much different from any of the previous waves of nativism: a mix of preoccupation over the economy, political and business interests, and fear of demographic change. Founding father Benjamin Franklin bluntly expressed this last concern with regard to German immigrants, who made up 30 percent of Pennsylvania's population, writing in the mid-eighteenth century: "Those who come hither are generally of the most ignorant Stupid Sort of their own Nation . . . and as few of the English understand the German Language, and so cannot address them either from the Press or Pulpit, 'tis almost impossible to remove any prejudices they once entertain. . . . Not being used to Liberty, they know not how to make a modest use of it.

"Unless the stream of their importation could be turned from this to other colonies, as you very judiciously propose, they will soon so out number us, that all the advantages we have will not in my opinion be able to preserve our language, and even our Government will be precarious," Franklin warned.[1]

Franklin's words have a familiar ring. But historians suggest that the real problem Franklin had with the Germans wasn't that he considered them a threat to the colony. He was miffed because his fledgling business printing publications in German, in particular the first German-language newspaper, the *Philadelphische Zeitung*, which he had launched in 1732, had failed after only one year.

History repeated itself with the twentieth-century nativists: Everyone has their own personal interests, and whoever is able to do so elevates them into a political, public interest. In 1994, the group in the Mexican restaurant in Orange County included several people whose personal histories and prejudices had brought them there that day.

One of the men there was Ron Prince, a forty-six year-old accountant from Tustin, California. According to press reports, Prince had first worked in a family business in Downey, a small city in southern California. But once the idea of pushing a ballot initiative to deny social services to illegal immigrants caught his attention, he threw himself wholeheartedly into the campaign. And after Proposition 187 was passed by voters on the November 1994 ballot, Prince enjoyed a successful career on the lecture circuit giving speeches on the subject across the country.

For years Prince has tirelessly dedicated himself to his mission. His most recent attempt to pass a measure denying public services to undocumented immigrants failed; he was unable to collect enough signatures to get it on the March 2006 California ballot. Despite his best efforts, Prince never recaptured the level of public interest he enjoyed in 1994.

DARK TIMES FOR THE SUNSHINE STATE

In the early 1990s, California was still feeling the effects of a recession that the rest of the country had already largely recovered from. The end of the Cold War had led to military base closings and cuts in the federal aerospace and defense budgets, cuts that had the strongest impact on California, with its large military and defense industry presence.

In the late 1980s, California shed some 800,000 jobs, the housing market collapsed, and for the first time in recent memory, official records indicated that more people were leaving the formerly prosperous state than arriving.[2] A budget deficit of $15 billion led to a tax hike.

With such a bleak outlook, it's easy to imagine how the record levels of immigration the state had experienced over the course of the previous decade—both legal and illegal—would be cause for concern for many Californians. The population of the state was rapidly diversifying, and the minority population was projected to grow at a faster rate than any other, thanks in large part to the arrival of immigrants.

This really irked Barbara Coe, who was also sitting at the table in the restaurant that day, perhaps enjoying some guacamole and tacos washed down with a few margaritas, a menu just as familiar to Californians as burgers and fries.

Coe has often publicly recounted how she had walked into a social services office in Orange County one day and saw how windows especially for Spanish and Vietnamese speakers were open, but the window for English speakers was closed. She described the scene as a little "United Nations," with many pregnant women speaking a dizzying array of different languages.[3]

It seems that that day was a turning point for Coe, in her sixties and about to retire from her job at the Anaheim Police Department. She vowed to fight against illegal immigrants, who, she was told by one of the employees at the social services offices, received more benefits than some citizens.

According to the law, undocumented immigrants could not receive anything beyond emergency room health care and, in California, prenatal care. Each state is free to decide how much health care it wants to cover, based on its resources and public health needs.

Education, however, is constitutionally mandated. According to the Supreme Court's 1982 decision in *Plyler v. Doe*,[4] no state can deny undocumented immigrant children the same free public education that is available to everyone else. The reasoning went that children should not be held responsible for their parents' actions and that basic education is too important for society as a whole to allow for the exclusion of certain categories of people. And the undocumented parents of children born in the United States can collect benefits, such as food stamps and WIC (Women, Infants, and Children), which provide nutrition assistance.

Hearing this was more than Coe could bear.

One of Coe's friends was Bill King, a former agent with the Immigration and Naturalization Service (INS). They soon formed a group they called Citizens for Action Now (CAN) and began holding meetings with like-minded people.

Coe and Prince met through CAN, and the chemistry between them was immediate. Prince, like Coe, told a personal story that had led him to join the struggle against undocumented immigrants. According to his story, an illegal immigrant from Canada who had been his friend and business partner had somehow ripped him off. (It was never exactly clear who had defrauded whom, since, according to public records, the only legal dispute between Prince and a former associate had involved a man who had resided legally in the country since the 1960s.)[5]

No matter his fuzzy motivations, Prince's idea to get an initiative on the ballot to punish undocumented immigrants in California was crystal clear. It was at the meeting at the Mexican restaurant that Prince, Coe, and King formed SOS.

Soon people with higher political profiles began flocking to the group. They included Assemblyman Richard Mountjoy, Republican from Arcadia and a couple of former high-level INS directors who were no strangers to controversy: Alan Nelson and Harold Ezell.

Nelson had ties to an organization called FAIR (Federation of Americans for Immigration Reform), a group that lobbied for the outright expulsion of undocumented immigrants and limits on legal immigration. The group has been linked to white supremacists.[6]

Ezell ran into trouble when, as western regional commissioner of the INS in the 1980s, he said publicly that illegal aliens should be "caught, skinned, and fried." He also commented that Californians supported Proposition 187 because "the people are tired of watching their state run wild and become a third world country."[7] At the same time, Ezell was donning a Mexican sombrero and promoting the 1986 IRCA in Latino neighborhoods.

The fledgling anti-immigration group did not have the funds to mount a serious statewide campaign. But luckily for SOS, its little ballot measure attracted the support of a very high-ranking individual with deep pockets and great political connections: Governor Pete Wilson, a Republican.

After four years as governor and in the middle of a painful recession, Wilson's approval ratings had dropped to their lowest levels as he sought reelection. According to an article in *California Journal*, Wilson had become "the most unpopular governor in the history of modern polling," with an approval rating of a mere 15 percent.[8]

As soon as Wilson decided to throw his support behind the measure proposed by SOS, later known as Proposition 187 everything changed. It was the perfect time for Wilson to wrap himself in the mantle of ultraconservatism and play to the basest passions of his party, whose ultraconservative and powerful wing had never considered him one of their own.

Before being elected governor, Wilson had been the mayor of San Diego and then a US senator. He had supported a woman's right to choose and had championed a program for farmers that would have facilitated bringing in workers from Mexico. But more than anything else, he was known for raising taxes to combat the deficit. He was not a knee-jerk conservative but a pragmatist.

As he launched his campaign for reelection, the Christian right exerted a powerful influence over the state's Republican Party. Their hatred for Wilson based on his support of women's choice was such that during a statewide Republican convention, they burned him in effigy so all the world could see exactly what they thought of their governor.

That deep-seated animosity faded once Wilson championed Proposition 187, insisting that California's myriad problems could be solved at least in part by denying public education and health care to the state's undocumented immigrants, who at the time comprised more than 1 million of California's 32 million inhabitants.

FROM 187 TO THE NEW FRONTIER

Proposition 187 triumphed at the polls in November 1994, with 63 percent of voters in favor and 37 percent opposed. Exit polls showed that the only ethnic group that voted consistently against it were Latinos: 77 percent voted against it and 23 percent in favor.

The majority of Latinos who voted against the measure clearly viewed it as aimed squarely against them, especially since Wilson's reelection campaign ads featured images of Mexicans streaming across the border willy-nilly. But the opposition of Latino voters was not enough to override the support of 63 percent of whites. Blacks and Asians were divided, with 47 percent voting for the measure and 53 percent opposing it. Interestingly, the parts of the state that were most accustomed to a diverse population—San Francisco, Alameda, and Los Angeles—were most opposed to Proposition 187.

Pete Wilson easily won a second term as governor, defeating a once-formidable adversary: Kathleen Brown, the sister and daughter of two legendary former Democratic governors.

And Wilson owed it all to the heated anti-immigrant sentiment that boiled over in California in the 1990s. Nevertheless, the decision to foment and capitalize on voters' fears of immigrants would have consequences for Wilson, Republicans, and immigrants themselves on a national level.

The first to sound the alarm on the consequences for the party were two highly respected conservative Republicans who adamantly opposed Proposition 187, talking over the rising hysteria in their own party that was then focused on public enemy number one: immigrants. William Bennett and Jack Kemp, two former cabinet members of the Reagan and Bush Sr. administrations, joined forces right before the November 1994 election to voice their opposition to Proposition 187 and to warn of the serious repercussions the measure's passage would have on the nation as a whole. The two conservative leaders issued a statement: "For some, immigrants have become a popular political and social scapegoat. But concerns about illegal immigration should not give rise to a series of fundamentally flawed, constitutionally questionable 'solutions' which are not consonant with our history."[9]

Kemp, a former housing secretary who was preparing for his presidential campaign in 1996—he would end up as Bob Dole's running mate—predicted how the controversial issue would play out when he warned his fellow Republicans: "I'm concerned that if Proposition 187 passes in California, it will be introduced in other states and people will want to put it in the 1996 [Republican] platform. It corrodes the soul of the party."[10]

Bennett, who was secretary of education under Reagan and considered an ultraconservative, went even further, saying that once something like Proposition 187 got started, everything would be viewed through the same lens. It was the wrong approach, according to Bennett, but it would become the standard protocol for dealing with all immigrants. In his view, it would poison democracy.[11]

Both men saw Proposition 187 as a threat to their staunchly conservative ideology, something the majority of their party failed to grasp. The proposition represented an expansion of government power, creating a kind of "Big Brother" state by transforming teachers, hospital staff, and other local employees into immigration agents. It was a profoundly anticonservative step.

The rest of the Republican Party moved to distance itself from Kemp and Bennett's position. Kemp was openly criticized at a function at the Richard Nixon Library a few weeks after his statements were made public. Some Republicans accused him of allying himself with the Democrats and President Bill Clinton, who, despite his own conservative views on immigration, officially opposed Proposition 187.

But everything that Kemp and Bennett predicted would happen did happen. Although most of Proposition 187's provisions never took effect—they were blocked by appeals courts—the vicious venom of nativism immediately took hold. Over time, other states tried to copy Proposition 187 while the Clinton administration worked to court independents in California during the 1996 election and struggled to silence the shrill voices of anti-immigrant hysteria in the state.

The Clinton White House knew what would come next: a rise in illegal immigration as a result of the policies of the North American Free Trade Alliance (NAFTA), which liberalized the markets of United States, Canada, and Mexico, eliminating trade barriers and made it impossible for Mexican corn farmers to compete with subsidized American corn. That single problem displaced thousands of Mexican farmers, and the jobs created in other industries were not enough to absorb them. Many emigrated from rural areas to cities in Mexico while others left for the United States.

This increased flow of Mexican immigrants across the border, combined with Clinton's relatively conservative views on immigration, led to a series of new federal operations meant to secure the border. The first was Operation Gatekeeper, initiated right before Proposition 187 was passed in the November 1994 California elections. One was a direct response to the other in Clinton's efforts to neutralize the issue politically.

Operation Gatekeeper was the first modern effort to reinforce a 2,000-mile border that had been guarded only halfheartedly until that time. In just two years, the budget of the INS doubled, as did the number of Border Patrol agents. The federal government began to install fences and other barriers along parts of the border, especially the most widely transited areas of illegal immigration between San Diego, Imperial Beach, and San Ysidro. Funds were also allocated to capture undocumented immigrants and the coyotes, or human traffickers, who brought them across the border.

DEADLY CROSSING

None of these actions made a dent in the flow of undocumented immigrants lured north by a rosy economic outlook. Almost immediately, their route across the border simply took a detour to more remote, far more dangerous areas of Arizona's unforgiving deserts and mountains. The number of immigrants who died in their attempt to cross the border escalated, and the business of human trafficking became more lucrative, as having a guide for this treacherous journey became increasingly necessary.

In the middle of his 1996 reelection campaign, President Clinton adopted a credo that another Democratic president, Barack Obama, would embrace years later. "Pro-immigrant on one side, and even tougher than some Republican administrations against undocumented immigration on the other" would be the unwritten manifesto of each. Clinton was publicly opposed to Proposition 187, but in his zeal to nurture a broad coalition of supporters, he fell back on strongly restrictionist measures to combat undocumented immigrants. Interestingly, illegal immigration was not an issue in his 1992 campaign—California would not put the issue on the map until Proposition 187 was introduced in 1994.

Policy makers and officials in the mid-1990s left a trail of blood in their wake. Crossing the border from Mexico into the United States had never been so perilous. Undocumented immigrants were not deterred, pressing onward over the Otay Mountains in San Diego County in California and down into the desert, which was freezing cold in winter and broiling hot in summer.

INS commissioner Doris Meissner said that the strategy was to discourage immigration in part by using geography as an "ally." In other words, immigration was not directly discouraged, but a harsh landscape definitely served its purpose: Between 1998 and 2004, an estimated two thousand men, women, and children died trying to cross the border. By comparison, in 1990, only nine were reported to have died in the attempt. Since the new border enforcement strategies were instituted in the 1990s, and according to the last count in 2009, at least five thousand migrants have died.[12]

Funneling migrants through the harsh Arizona mountains and deserts eventually would have another effect: The increase in illegal crossings would create in that state an ideal environment for rising anti-immigrant sentiment. This tactic culminated in the passage of Arizona Senate Bill 1070 in 2010, the first law that attempted to authorize a state's enforcement of immigration law as if Arizona were a sovereign nation.

After Proposition 187 was passed in 1994, the immigration issue played out just as Bennett and Kemp had anticipated: A dark bile permeated into the heartland of the country, making it virtually impossible to have a reasonable public dialogue on the issue for nearly two decades.

THREE

NATIVISM
THE OLD AND THE NEW

The working people in America are not in a thoroughly prosperous condition, and there are already many out of employment. We would be glad to welcome the distressed people of all nations, but it must be admitted, under existing circumstances, the wholesale immigration from the Old World is not the unmixed blessing it was so long held to be.

—Editorial from the *New Orleans Picayune*, 1880

We heartily approve all legitimate efforts to prevent the United States from being used as the dumping ground for the known criminals and professional paupers of Europe; and we demand the rigid enforcement of the laws against Chinese immigration and the importation of foreign workmen under contract, to degrade American labor and lessen its wages.

—Democratic Party platform, 1892

We favor the enactment of more stringent laws and regulations for the restriction of criminal, pauper and contract immigration.

—Republican Party platform, 1892

It is said . . . that the quality of recent immigration is undesirable. The time is quite within recent memory when the same thing was said of immigrants who, with their descendants, are now numbered among our best citizens.

—President Grover Cleveland[1]

BETWEEN 1836 AND 1914, SOME 30 MILLION IMMIGRANTS CAME TO THE UNITED States from Europe. At the time, there were no immigration limits at all, and practically anyone from the Old Country who made the transatlantic crossing hoping to start a new life was accepted, unless they were gravely ill.

America had not yet established specific quotas for how many people from a particular country would be allowed in, with the notable exception of the Chinese. The United States Congress passed the Chinese Exclusion Act in 1882 to prevent immigrants from China from ever becoming naturalized citizens, the only country to ever have a special law restricting immigration of its citizens to the United States.

Workers from China had begun arriving in the mid-nineteenth century, attracted by abundant jobs constructing the transcontinental railroad and by the gold rush. They were viewed as a burden and as competition for low-wage, low-skilled jobs, which, it was feared, would not be in such great supply once the railroad was finished and the mines ran out of gold.

The Chinese Exclusion Act was the only legal restriction in an otherwise open immigration policy that had existed since the country's founding until Congress established quotas in 1924. Illegal immigration did not technically exist for anyone until that year, since almost everyone was admitted.

According to records on Ellis Island, the nation's busiest port of entry for millions of immigrants between 1892 and 1954, only about 2 percent of the arrivals that came through the Island in the first few decades of its use were sent back to their country of origin after being screened for incurable illness, disabilities, or evidence of criminal background. That means that 98 percent of those who arrived by boat were admitted into the country. To claim that one's own ancestors who immigrated from another country at that time were "legal," and therefore different from or better than today's immigrants, is ludicrous. Historically, there was no such thing as illegal immigration prior to 1924.

One thing that has remained constant in the ever-evolving state of immigration over the centuries is the persistent sense that the latest wave of immigrants, whoever they may be, are ruining the country—at least according to the previous, more established group of immigrants.

In the mid-1800s, for example, the Know Nothing movement came to prominence. With membership open only to Protestant males of British extraction, the nativist group viewed German and Irish Catholic immigrants as a dangerous threat.

From 1880 onward, especially after a series of recessions rocked the national economy beginning in 1882, more serious attempts were made to formally prohibit immigrants from certain countries from coming to America. The political rhetoric and public unease was focused on newcomers from southern and eastern Europe (Italy, Hungary, and Russia), who represented a different kind of immigrant from previous, now-established groups who had come to the United States from England, Germany, and Sweden and other Nordic countries.

In 1894, three young Harvard College graduates formed the Immigration Restriction League to oppose the "undesirable" immigrants from southern and eastern Europe who supposedly posed a "threat" to the American lifestyle and were driving down wages. The league worried that the "new immigrants" brought poverty and crime with them, especially in times of high unemployment.[2]

One of the league's more prominent members was Francis Walker, the superintendent of the United States Census and president of the prestigious Massachusetts Institute of Technology. In her book *Illegal Aliens and the Making of Modern America,*

Columbia University history professor Mae Ngai explains that Walker was a social Darwinist who believed there were good immigrants and bad immigrants—not because some were upstanding, hardworking citizens and some were criminals, but solely because of their nationality. Walker believed that immigrants from Italy, Hungary, Austria, and Russia were "vast masses of peasants, of the lowest, most degraded possible origins, defeated men who represented the most abject failure in the struggle for existence."[3]

The nineteenth century, especially the latter half, was a time of large-scale immigration into the United States due to improvements in transportation—faster steam ships with cheaper fares—and farming, which displaced populations in southern and eastern Europe. But the immigrant communities that were already established in the United States began to wonder if there weren't already enough poor, struggling people in the "land of opportunity" trying to make a better life. The nation was industrializing and growing, but it was far from being a world superpower. At that time, groups like the Immigration Restriction League lobbied Congress, and labor unions supported establishing laws and protocols that would limit immigration.

Although technically there were no legal and illegal immigrants at the time, people began thinking of certain groups as "desirables" and "undesirables." The latter group was categorized as such because of their levels of poverty and education, religion or country of origin, and because of the perceived effect their arrival would have on salaries and the economic health of the country as a whole.

In an interview for this book, Ngai compared the current wave of anti-immigrant feelings that began to surge in the mid-1990s with the backlash that took place in the late 1800s and early 1900s. According to Ngai, what we are experiencing now is very similar to what happened then. In both periods, there was a large influx of immigrants who were viewed as fundamentally different from the groups of immigrants who had preceded them. They were seen as dirty and diseased, bringing crime along with them, and unwilling to learn English or assimilate.[4]

Over time, those fears proved to be totally unfounded. Each wave of "undesirable" immigrants has gone through its own process of integration and become part of the fabric of the United States, each group contributing to the nation's progress.

Today critics of immigration draw a clear distinction between immigrants of the turn of the twentieth century and the current wave and between legal and illegal immigration. "My ancestors came to this country *legally*" is a common refrain in conversations attempting to define who is an acceptable immigrant and who is not.

In the early 1920s new laws established quotas, which mainly aimed to limit the number of Jews, Italians, and Slavs who could enter the country. The numerical limits established by law had the effect of promoting immigration from countries with populations that were considered "white," which at the time meant, for the most part, Anglo-Saxon Protestants. Some would-be immigrants were deemed ineligible strictly on the basis of race.

With the passage of those restrictive laws came the first legal proceedings for deporting foreigners, which effectively created the country's first illegal immigrants. The border with Mexico was virtually open, with unrestricted passage at this time. All of the attention was focused on "indigent" immigrants from Europe.

In her book on the history of illegal immigration, Ngai wrote:

> Immigration inspectors ignored Mexicans coming into the south-western United States during the 1900s and 1910s to work in railroad construction, mining and agriculture. The Immigration Bureau did not seriously consider Mexican immigration within its purview but rather as something that was regulated by labor market demands in the

southwestern border states. The Immigration Act of 1917 [a first step in restricting the pace of immigration], doubled the head tax [paid by immigrants] and imposed a literacy test, erecting the first barriers to entry, but unlawful entry was limited, as the Labor Department exempted Mexicans from the requirements during the war.[5]

ONE HUNDRED YEARS LATER

Ever since those first immigration restrictions, the general public's attitude and the laws addressing immigration have fluctuated along with the overall mood of the country. The wave of stringent laws against illegal immigrants that began in the mid-1990s came about because of prevailing views on race and what the racial composition of America should be, an uncertain economic outlook, and politics.

Anti-immigrant rhetoric has hardly changed over the past century. Although today's harshest critics like to stress that immigrants who enter the country without authorization are lawbreakers, the overriding sentiments were exactly the same in the days before illegal immigration existed: Fear of radical demographic change; fear that local culture or the "American way of life" will be altered; fears of increased competition for scarce jobs and depression of wages, disease, and the social chaos that undocumented immigrants supposedly bring with them are the same arguments used in times past, slightly updated for the modern age.

And today's politicians use these well-worn arguments effectively.

"Of course we are a nation of immigrants, and our generosity towards immigrants will continue. But our current immigration laws are broken and must be fixed. When 40 percent of the births in the public hospitals of our most populous state, California, are to illegal aliens; when the number of illegal aliens entering our country every three years could populate a city the size of Boston or Dallas or San Francisco, when half the five million illegal aliens in the US today use fraudulent documents to illegally obtain jobs and welfare benefits, it's not a problem, it's a crisis," wrote Republican congressman from Texas Lamar Smith in a 1996 opinion piece published in several newspapers across the country.[6]

Smith trotted out three arguments that have withstood the test of time. Immigrants—now called illegal immigrants—are increasing too rapidly; they are criminals and are taking advantage of the social welfare system. You could say that solemnly venerating America's tradition of accepting the immigrants of old while sounding alarm bells about the crises caused by the entirely unacceptable current generation of immigrants is a proud tradition of US politics. But the solutions that have been prescribed have not cured the disease that is the "immigration problem," if any solution even exists, which is open to debate.

Smith was the principal author of the Illegal Immigration Reform and Immigrant Responsibility Act (IIRIRA), which was passed in 1996. After the success of Proposition 187 in California, the blatant exploitation of anti-immigrant fears became a blueprint for political success. Other politicians soon followed Wilson's example.

According to Kevin Johnson,[7] dean of the School of Law at the University of California at Davis, who studies the issue, Wilson and the California residents who supported Proposition 187 wanted to send a message to the federal government that they were worried about illegal immigration. The feds got the message loud and clear.

By 1996, the issue had an added political dimension. Two years earlier, in the midterm elections, dissatisfaction with Bill Clinton had given Republicans a majority in the House of Representatives for the first time in decades. Now it was time for another presidential election, and although Clinton had opposed Proposition 187, he instituted a series of border control measures, such as Operation Gatekeeper, which were designed to placate voters concerned about immigration, especially those in California.

In Congress, Republicans in the House, led by Majority leader Newt Gingrich, worked to pass a series of measures that they had not been able to push through when they were the minority party. One initiative was overhauling welfare, and the other was immigration.

In the mid-1990s, the United States experienced strong economic growth. Many new jobs were added in the service sector, attracting both legal and illegal immigrants. The Immigration and Reform Act of 1986 was in effect, but, as has already been discussed, without meaningful sanctions levied against employers of undocumented workers, the Act was not sufficient to deter the flow of immigrants north. The wars that ravaged Central America in the 1980s and the ensuing flood of refugees and asylum seekers did the rest, and the United States had its most recent major increase in the flow of immigration.

Politicians fully exploited the rising backlash against foreigners to build support for particular candidates and platforms. After all, those same politicians had played a key role in fomenting the public's xenophobic sentiments.

Sherry Bebitch Jeffe, political analyst and senior fellow at the School of Policy, Planning and Development at the University of Southern California, explains: "There appear to be a myriad of reasons for these attitudes. In times of economic crisis, people look for scapegoats. Also, the perception that if it has worked before it will continue to work in the future is very important in politics."[8]

In spite of the strong economy, President Clinton was under attack by Republicans on all fronts: His personal life, his failed health care reform, and alleged corruption in his administration were all the focus of intense scrutiny. Clinton was persecuted and repeatedly investigated for the Whitewater case, Travelgate, the death of deputy White House counsel Vince Foster, and, last but not least, his relationship with White House intern Monica Lewinsky.

Because he was under siege, as his campaign for reelection got under way in 1996 Clinton was willing to adopt a more moderate posture on immigration—or some would say a more hardline position. On September 30, 1996, Clinton signed into law the IIRIRA. He had previously unveiled a series of operations to strengthen border security and supported and strengthened specific legal reforms passed that year that would result in increasingly faster deportations of immigrants for many years to come, including legal immigrants who had committed minor infractions of the law.

"The immigration law of 1996 was the most stringent legislation of its kind in modern US history. It reduced judicial review, deportations and detentions were increased, the options for asylum seekers were restricted, and it required citizens who sponsor immigrants to prove they could support them if need be," Johnson said.

Repercussions of the 1996 law can still be felt. Hundreds of thousands of immigrants, including legal residents who could have had a scrape with the law in the past—for example, a driving under the influence conviction—were arrested and jailed, and many were deported.

"We are seeing an increasing number of legal permanent residents convicted of nonviolent offenses, some of which occurred decades ago, who under the new law must be detained and removed from the country," Doris Meissner, head of the Immigration and Naturalization Service (INS) during the Clinton administration, said in 2000.[9] Meissner was in charge of enforcing the law, but in

1996 she published an article criticizing it as excessive: "Instead of having the discretion to grant relief in appropriate cases, immigration judges and INS officers are now finding that there are many cases in which their hands are tied," she observed.[10]

The number of Border Patrol agents was doubled, and asylum seekers were forcibly detained if they could not prove immediately upon entering the country that they had a credible fear of persecution in their home country—a very tall order for someone who had just escaped from a difficult situation and now faced armed US officials at an official point of entry.

Although the 1996 law effectively limited the legal rights of potential immigrants, there was one thing it did not do: stop or slow down the flow of unauthorized immigration, especially during good economic times.

The number of undocumented immigrants in the United States, estimated at 5 million in 1996, had more than doubled fifteen years later. Once again, the rhetoric had no effect on the reality. And once again, tough-talking politicians started to bat around solutions that did nothing to mitigate illegal immigration over the long term.

PART II
THE RADICALIZATION OF ANTI-IMMIGRANT LAWS AND LEGAL CHAOS

FOUR
THE NEW MILLENNIUM
BUSH, LATINOS, AND 9/11

IN ITS SEPTEMBER 7, 2001 ISSUE, JUST DAYS BEFORE THE 9/11 ATTACKS, *Time* magazine honored Mexican president Vicente Fox as its "Person of the Week." Talking about his three-day visit to Washington the previous week, the piece observed: "There's something charmingly Quixotic about a Mexican President ambling into the White House in cowboy boots and urging his host to make the most profound change in decades to U.S. immigration law—and to do it before Christmas. But Vicente Fox is nothing if not Quixotic. . . . And right now, the former Coca-Cola executive's ability to deliver is dependent in no small part on his special relationship with President George W. Bush."

That was the reality in Washington in the days before the terrorist attacks that would change everything in ways no one could predict. Bush and Fox both had their own reasons for trying to enact an immigration reform that would have legalized a significant number of undocumented immigrants then working and living "up north." But as we all know now, those efforts to construct permanent reform, painted in folksy terms, such as the goal of Secretary of Foreign Relations for Mexico Jorge Castaneda of achieving "the whole enchilada," or the complete legalization of millions of undocumented workers, are now merely a distant memory. Given the current political climate, it's hard to believe that such high-level, serious discussions on the issue were possible not so long ago.

Ten years after 9/11 attacks, the perspective is very different. Not only is there no serious discussion at any level regarding the proverbial "enchilada," members of the immigrant community must now content themselves with any meager scraps that may get thrown their way. By 2011, the political class had abandoned any meaningful dialogue that would address how to fully integrate the millions of undocumented immigrants already here into this country's economic and social fabric, even though the reality is that they are firmly entrenched anyway. In many ways, the economic and social future of this country will rest, in no small part, on the decisions that will be made affecting the immigrants already here and those to come.

In the late summer of 2001, there was a real sense of optimism. It's not that there was a euphoric, overwhelmingly pro-immigrant sentiment sweeping the nation, but the United States and Mexico were engaged in positive exchanges on what the solution to the immigration issue should be. The cautiously hopeful outlook at the turn of the millennium can be attributed largely to the policy positions of President George W. Bush. Before arriving at the White House in 2000, Bush had spent six years as governor of Texas, a state with strong economic and personal ties with its southern neighbor. Governor Bush spoke rudimentary Spanish, learned during his time in Texas, he had a Mexican sister-in-law (Columba, his brother Jeb's wife), and genuinely believed that the future of the Republican Party depended on a vision of "compassionate conservatism."

At the time, Bush also believed that the anti-Latino, anti-immigrant attitude espoused by other prominent Republicans—beginning with Governor Pete Wilson in California and spreading like wildfire—would only drag the party down over the long run. Bush was influenced by his relationships with the Mexican American community in Texas and by the counsel he received from Lionel Sosa, a political consultant who had worked on Ronald Reagan's winning presidential campaign in 1980.

When Reagan asked Sosa, a publicist in San Antonio, to help him win the Latino vote in 1980, he uttered the phrase that many other Republicans would borrow when they wanted to show that the Latin American community's natural sympathies lay with their party. Reagan told Sosa that "Hispanics are Republicans, they just don't know it yet."

Sosa understood what many other Republican strategists seem to have forgotten, or at least ignored, when they opted for short-term results instead of long-term strategy: Latinos were just like any other group of voters; they could sympathize with for the goals of any party, as long as they felt included, respected, and valued. At the very least, they didn't want to feel attacked or insulted, which is exactly what many Latinos sensed from the Republican Party in later years, beginning the mid-1990s and well into the twenty-first century.

Latinos, Mexicans, and Mexican Americans in particular were naturally conservative, Reagan reasoned, and Sosa agreed. They were family oriented, very religious, with a strong work ethic, and self-sufficient. But somebody else had gotten to this group of voters first, back in the 1960s: John F. Kennedy and Robert Kennedy, during their respective presidential campaigns.

The fight for civil rights and the role that President Kennedy and then Lyndon Johnson had in passing the Civil Rights Act in 1965, and later the support that Robert Kennedy offered to migrant workers and Cesar Chavez and the United Farm Workers union, made the Democrats the party of choice for Latino voters. First Lady Jacqueline Kennedy made television commercials in Spanish for her husband's presidential campaign in 1960. After he was elected, the couple made a state visit to Mexico, where they were received like royalty.

And because of their position, generally on the lower rungs of the socioeconomic ladder, and their community-oriented culture, most Latinos gravitated to traditionally Democratic views on social issues. That has not changed to this day. Numerous studies have concluded that in strictly political terms, a majority of Latino immigrants in the United States can be considered liberal on the US ideological scale. Notable exceptions are Cubans and Nicaraguans, the latter of whom arrived in the United States in the 1980s having fled the leftist Castro and Sandinista governments, and were given asylum by the American government.

Over and over again in opinion polls, Latinos have clearly expressed their conviction that government has an important role to play in ensuring the well-being of society; they tend to believe that abortion and religion are private, not political issues; and although they are incurably optimistic about their own possibilities for achieving relative success, they do not delude themselves about their prospects for being as rich as Donald Trump or Warren Buffett someday, as low-income, non-Hispanic whites tend to do.

However, there is a subset of fiscal and social conservatives within the Latino community. Those conservative tendencies tend to be reinforced as they ascend the social ladder or, in the case of immigrants, integrate more fully into various aspects of society. Under the right circumstances, this group can come to genuinely identify with the Republican Party.

Political consultant Sosa focused his efforts on that segment of the community in 1980, when he helped Reagan to win between 37 and 44 percent of the Latino vote. At that time, the Latino population as a whole was much smaller than it is today, and its vote did not have the impact it would have in later decades, but the seed had been planted. Sosa recognized that the growing Latino vote would play an important role in future elections. And he was not wrong, although progress would be slow.

In their rise to power, the Bush brothers—George W.'s younger brother Jeb had become governor of Florida in 1999—appeared to be moderates on issues considered typically Latino, especially immigration; in contrast, other Republicans followed California governor Pete Wilson's lead and loudly called for restrictive measures against immigrants, careful to draw the distinction between "illegal" (bad) and "legal" (good) immigration.

Wilson's strategy had the desired effect on his reelection campaign, but it left a bad impression on California's growing Latino population. The television commercials that would prove to play a critical role in Pete Wilson's reelection also made him one of the most hated politicians among California's Latino immigrant community. In a larger context, Wilson and his aggressive campaign against undocumented immigrants made a serious and lasting impression on American politics across the country that would transcend the campaign of 1994 and foster an increasingly tense atmosphere openly hostile to undocumented immigrants over the next fifteen years.

The best-known television ad would also do the most damage to the Republican Party's reputation in the minds of Latino voters. In the ad's first few seconds, the camera focuses on a border checkpoint, and a sign reading "Mexico" is clearly visible. The footage has a grainy look, as if it were captured by a surveillance camera. There is an orderly line of vehicles heading south, patiently waiting to enter Mexico, while groups of people on foot chaotically cross the border in the opposite direction, streaming past the lines of cars, running frantically. The voiceover narrator sounds like something out of a horror movie: "*And they keep coming . . . the federal government won't stop them at the border, yet requires us to pay billions of dollars to take care of them,*" the voice intones.

With that one ad, Wilson defined and stoked the fears of a segment of the population about the growing presence of immigrants in their midst, especially Mexicans and Central Americans, who had arrived by the hundreds of thousands in the 1980s. The previously unspoken dread was now made visually evident: aliens were running rampant across the border, overwhelming the country, straining its economy, promoting illegality and chaos, all at enormous taxpayer expense. Their positive contributions to the American economy and culture were not alluded to at all, nor were their reasons for crossing the border. It was a bold campaign strategy, and it worked like a charm.

In November 1994, voters passed Proposition 187 as a referendum. (The measure was intended to deny health care, public education, and social services to undocumented immigrants and would require social service workers to check the immigration status of anyone applying for benefits.) Subsequently Pete Wilson was reelected to serve as governor for four more years. That election had an unintended consequence: It provoked an intense reaction among Latino voters, who would reject Republican candidates at the polls over and over again in the following years and elect a historic number of Latinos to public office. In 2003, California elected its first Democratic governor in twenty years.

Meanwhile, in Texas, gubernatorial candidate George W. Bush refused to follow the example of other Republicans and rejected calls to support Proposition 187 or similar measures. His brother Jeb, running for governor in Florida, also did not jump on the anti-immigrant bandwagon, although he lost his campaign. In 1994, George W. Bush became governor of Texas and four years later, in 1998, Jeb won the governorship in Florida, and George was reelected in Texas. The position of both brothers, standing apart from the hard-liners on immigration within their own party, had been established.

George W. Bush was elected President of the United States in November 2000. The traumatic process involved a recount of votes in Florida and a Supreme Court decision, which, to many critics, called into question the validity of his victory. But he had definitely won 35 percent of the Latino vote, a considerable percentage and the highest achieved by any Republican candidate since Ronald Reagan.

His first months in office were relatively calm. President Bush was intent on improving relations with Mexico and in turn, gathering increasing support from the Latino population in the United States. Therefore, one of his highest priorities was to focus on US relations with Mexico and an agreement on immigration, which he had been in the midst of discussing with President Fox less than a week before two passenger planes crashed into the Twin Towers in New York, another plane slammed into the Pentagon, and a fourth, en route to the White House, crashed in a field in Pennsylvania.

One direct consequence of the terrorist attacks was that the possibility of immigration reform and the eventual legalization of undocumented immigrants evaporated instantly. Bush's presidency can be divided into two parts: before 9/11 and after 9/11. On the morning of the attacks, Bush was at an elementary school in Sarasota, Florida, reading to a group of children as photographers and cameramen captured the moment. We can't know exactly what ran through the president's mind in the minutes that ticked by after White House Chief of Staff Andrew Card stepped into the classroom and whispered, "America is under attack." What is crystal clear looking back is that his presidency changed completely in that instant. Soon his administration would focus on "the war on terror" above all else.

Immigration politics and the general public's attitude toward foreigners would suffer drastic changes as a result of the 9/11 attacks. The people most affected would not be terrorists, against whom new regulations would prove to have a minimal effect—ten years after the attacks, only thirty-seven individuals have been expelled because of suspicions of terrorist activity. Hundreds of thousands of innocent, undocumented workers, however, have been deported.

FIVE
IMMIGRATION
A QUESTION OF NATIONAL SECURITY

IN 1901, LEON CZOLGOSZ, THE SON OF POLISH IMMIGRANTS, ASSASSINATED President William McKinley at the Temple of Music in Buffalo, New York. The president had been there to take part in the Pan-American Exposition. Although Czolgosz had been born in the United States, Congress reacted to the assassination by passing the Immigration Act of 1903, also known as the Anarchist Exclusion Act, which barred the entry of anarchists and anyone who espoused attacking the government by force or violence or by assassinating political leaders.

It is not clear how such a law might have prevented McKinley's assassination. The anarchist in question was native born, and his parents, like so many others, were immigrant workers who had come to the United States to escape the poverty and oppression of their native countries in the mid- to late 1800s, before there were any restrictions on European immigration.

But that was hardly the first time the United States had responded to acts of violence committed on its soil—or to less specific fears or paranoia about a broader threat—by passing laws that restricted the entry of foreigners. These laws began in 1798 in the United States, when war with France was feared. Anticipating this, Congress passed the Alien and Sedition Acts. The Alien Act, passed on June 25, allowed the president to deport foreigners "dangerous to the peace and safety of the United States" during peacetime. The Alien Enemies Act, passed on July 6, authorized the detention and deportation of aliens determined to be "a danger of the public peace and safety" during wartime.

Do these laws have a familiar ring? A very similar provision was included in the USA Patriot Act (formally known as Uniting and Strengthening America by Providing Appropriate Tools Required to Intercept and Obstruct Terrorism Act of 2001), passed in October 2001, barely a month after the terrorist attacks of 9/11. The Patriot Act—a moniker that could have been dreamed up by the advertising geniuses on Madison Avenue—included what was called "enhanced immigration provisions." In a section that has a nineteenth-century feel, the US Attorney General is granted the exceptional power to detain foreigners indefinitely if they are reasonably considered to be "a national security threat."

And so it has gone throughout US history. The Chinese Exclusion Act and the detention of Japanese Americans in "legal" concentration camps after the attack on Pearl Harbor are notable episodes in the ongoing saga of America's suspicion and distrust of foreigners. The image of a threatening outsider is a provocative one to any peoples or culture, but it is especially interesting, and absurd, when the majority of that particular culture are descendants of foreigners who came here just a few generations ago.

Between 1882 and 1943, the immigration of Chinese people was completely prohibited by US law. The Chinese Exclusion Act had nothing to do with terrorism; it had everything to do with preventing Chinese immigrants from exercising their well-known penchant to travel to the farthest reaches of the globe in search of economic opportunity and to perform backbreaking labor for very low wages.

As long as the Chinese were needed to do the hardest jobs the country had to offer—such as constructing the transcontinental railroad—their presence was grudgingly tolerated. They were allowed to live together in ghettos, ghettos that eventually developed into today's wonderfully vibrant Chinatowns in cities across the country.

But when it seemed there were enough Chinese in the country—and when the railroad was built and the gold mines were exhausted—legislators not only sought to regulate immigration patterns of this particular group but also passed laws barring them from entering the country under any circumstances and preventing those already here from becoming US citizens. This legal exclusion of an entire ethnic group lasted for more than sixty years. This chapter in the history of the United States is rarely mentioned in the romanticized narrative of the country that many Americans like to tell themselves, of a nation built by hardworking immigrants and their descendants coming together in the melting pot of the New World.

What happened to the Japanese was even more deplorable, although because of the widespread paranoia gripping the nation at the time, the restrictive measures seemed perfectly acceptable to most Americans. In effect, hundreds of thousands of Japanese Americans, many of whom had been born in the United States and almost all of whom had nothing to do with Emperor Hirohito's army, were isolated and confined in ten concentration camps across the country.

In her book *Impossible Subjects: Illegal Aliens and the Making of Modern America*, history professor and immigration expert Mae M. Ngai explains that what happened to Japanese Americans during World War II is "the most extreme case" in American history of punitive acts perpetrated by the government against people who, in spite of being mostly American citizens, were treated like foreign enemies.[1] Ngai asserts that although the government did not formally nullify the US citizenship of Japanese Americans, the practical effect of the treatment they received, based solely on their race, amounted to the same thing. The government assumed that all Japanese were disloyal to the United States. So 120,000 people were arrested, two-thirds of whom were US citizens, and were taken far from their homes on the West Coast and imprisoned in ten concentration camps in the interior of the country.

With the passage of time, most of these "security" measures have been overturned by the courts and sharply criticized for often overreaching their authority. The judicial branch of the government is the only one that seems to operate with at least the appearance of objectivity, although it is also subject to political influence since federal judges are nominated by the sitting president.

Fast forward to the start of the new millennium, and the tendencies of the past repeated themselves. The shock of the terrorist attacks of September 11, 2001 produced responses that would exert an effect as strong as a volcanic eruption on immigration policy over the next decade.

Immediately after the attacks, committed by nineteen terrorists from Saudi Arabia, Libya, Egypt, and the United Arab Emirates who entered the country legally with valid visas, the US government began making changes to immigration law that profoundly affected regular immigrants much more so than any potential terrorists.

A good example of these type of actions were the sweeps of undocumented workers—called Operation Tarmac, these sweeps were conducted at airports and at people's homes, beginning in December 2001 and continuing for the next several months— and the passage of a law just a few weeks after the 9/11 attacks that created the new Transportation Security Authority. The TSA would be responsible for handling and screening luggage as well as screening passengers, a service that until that time had been subcontracted out to private companies who generally paid their employees the minimum wage.

In the wake of the attacks, immediate measures were taken against immigrants from Arab countries—such as requiring all men from a list of Arabic countries and of a certain age to register with the federal government. The Department of Justice (DOJ), headed by Republican John Ashcroft, also set to work to crack down on airports and other places of high importance to the country, such as military bases, historic sites, and nuclear power plants, and rid them of all unauthorized workers because of the supposed threat these workers posed to the country.

"Unauthorized" meant undocumented immigrants, who were employed on airplane maintenance crews, as cleaning staff, in food service, and in other support positions.

Attorney General Ashcroft, known for his bizarre insistence on covering up the seminude statues that had adorned the Great Hall of the DOJ since 1930 because he did not like to be photographed in front of them, made numerous statements characterizing airport workers as a threat to national security, even though not one was ever accused of any terrorist-related charge or was ever even under suspicion.

"These individuals are charged with gaining access to secure areas of our airports by lying on security applications, using false or fictitious Social Security numbers or committing various immigration frauds," Ashcroft said at a press conference, commenting on Operation Tarmac's success.[2]

According to the Government Accountability Office, by 2004, 195 airports had been investigated and 607 unauthorized employees had been identified. Of those, 30 percent were classified as having overstayed visas with which they had legally entered the country. The other 70 percent were undocumented immigrants who had crossed over the border by land.[3]

These classifications were important to the authorities because, according to the DOJ, three of the terrorists had violated the terms of their temporary visas. Following this logic, other foreigners who were in the country illegally, especially those with access to secure areas at airports or other critical infrastructure facilities, and who had violated the terms of their visas or illegally crossed the border, had to be prosecuted to the fullest extent of the law.

Operation Tarmac was considered a success, and similar sweeps were applied to workers of the Winter Olympic Games in Salt Lake City in 2002 and the Super Bowl in San Diego in 2003. During the sweep conducted for the Super Bowl, seventy-nine unauthorized workers were discovered within the security perimeters of the stadium.

Additionally, following new laws passed just a few weeks after 9/11, a new method to "protect the homeland" was instituted: All airport workers from then on had to be US citizens. Hundreds of legal permanent residents were fired from their jobs. As had happened many other times throughout US history, the patriotism and morality of everyday working people was suddenly under suspicion, their only transgression not having yet gone through the naturalization process to become citizens.

Meanwhile, as the maintenance staff who cleaned the bathrooms at the airports were closely scrutinized, the Immigration and Naturalization Service (INS) committed an egregious error, which the country promptly forgot about in its zeal for patriotic unity. Six months after the terrorist attacks, a flight school in Venice, Florida, received a letter from the INS stating that Mohamed Atta and Marwan al-Shehhi, two of the terrorists who had died on 9/11 (according to most accounts, Atta was the leader of the group), had been granted a change in visa status from "tourist" to "student." They had, albeit posthumously, received permission from the government to remain in the country and study at the school.

PROFOUND EFFECTS ON IMMIGRATION POLITICS

In the first few months following 9/11, the dark shadow of perceived threats to national security was invoked over and over again in discussions about the alarming state of security at the border and the troubling presence of undocumented immigrants already in the country.

"[The September 11, 2001 terrorist attacks] had a profound impact on immigrants and U.S. immigration policy," states Stephen Yale Loehr, a professor at the Cornell University School of Law. "Overall, the U.S. government overemphasized the use of the immigration system to try to combat terrorism. Instead of using anti-terrorism laws, we often use minor immigration violations to arrest people, with only limited success. That only gave the nation a false sense of security [that as long as the wrong people were kept out or deported everything would be okay]."[4]

The terrorist attacks of 9/11 changed the debate over the way immigration laws in the country were applied. The country's attitude as a whole toward immigrants was transformed, and any opportunity for enacting meaningful immigration reform was lost for at least a decade. A new image of the United States as less open to foreigners took root around the world.

According to Idean Salehyan, professor of political science at the University of North Texas and an expert in immigration law and political asylum, "Probably the biggest symbolic change was the total reorganization of the government institutions responsible for immigration control. From having an agency [the INS] in charge of immigration within the Department of Justice, they created the huge Department of Homeland Security, and with that, created various agencies to deal with immigration, such as Immigration and Customs Enforcement (ICE), US Citizenship and Immigration Services, US Customs and Border Protection, and others."[5]

Immigration went from being defined as an issue of justice to one of national security. The effect of this fundamental change in perception was that not only were immigrants from Arab and Middle Eastern countries "under suspicion" in the wake of the attacks, but all foreigners who could potentially come into the country and those undocumented immigrants who were already in our midst were now subject to intense scrutiny.

At the same time, the discussion about comprehensive immigration reform that had been progressing steadily with Bush's election to the presidency came to a dead stop. Remember that in the months leading up to 9/11, Bush and Mexican president Vicente Fox had been holding high-level meetings to find common ground on the issue and to introduce immigration reform into Congress.

"We don't have a crystal ball to prove it, but I truly believe those meetings could have resulted in very positive progress toward some kind of immigration reform," asserts Brooklyn Law School professor Maryellen Fullerton. "Without doubt there were and will always be political forces opposed to it, but it's also certain that after 9/11 they were able to radically change the tone of the debate."[6]

And Congress acted quickly. It's not accurate to say that laws relating to immigration stopped dead in those years. Indeed, any chance of immigration reform with legalization appeared to be dead, but between 2001 and 2006, Congress and President Bush passed six measures that included new restrictions on entering and remaining in the country.

The first was introduced in Congress just eight days after 9/11, a piece of legislation called the Anti-Terrorism Act of 2001. It was soon followed by the Patriot Act, a controversial measure that expanded the government's powers to investigate citizens and foreigners alike. It strengthened and expanded the government's abilities to gather domestic intelligence and detect and combat the financing of terrorist groups, and it facilitated the deportation of those suspected of being terrorists. It also allowed for the indefinite detention of certain categories of noncitizen suspects.

A few months later, Congress passed yet another law: the Enhanced Border Security and Visa Reform Act. This law created a system now known as US-VISIT, which required all foreigners entering the country to register their biometric information with the government while imposing additional requirements on foreign students.

Then in 2005 came the Real ID Act, which among other things established new federal standards for driver's licenses issued by the states, including banning driver's licenses for all undocumented immigrants (a new federal mandate). Most states in the country issued drivers licenses without regard to legal immigration status before that.

The process of applying for residency and naturalization became much more arduous for those who legally entered the country as a visitor, student, or worker on a temporary visa because the background checks that all applicants were subject to were in much more depth than had been required before 9/11.

"Thousands of immigrants, asylum seekers, and refugees had to wait much longer to enter the United States," according to Loehr. "And special registration programs were instituted for the entry and exit of nationals from a list of twenty-six countries, which were eliminated a few years later because they had no real effect."[7]

In 2005, Congress began what was as of this writing the last major attempt to pass comprehensive immigration reform. Experts believe that the post-9/11 mood heavily influenced the results. And the upcoming midterm elections of 2006 exerted some pressure on many Congressmen and women.

A report from the Migratory Policy Institute published in August 2011 concluded that the attacks of 9/11 led to a radical vision of how the laws should be applied. This view resulted in the passage of the highly restrictive Border Protection, Antiterrorism, and Illegal Immigration Control Act of 2005 in the House of Representatives, setting off the massive pro-immigrant marches in major cities across the country. The bill did not pass in the Senate. Then in 2006 and 2007, attempts to introduce comprehensive immigration reform in Congress failed.

According to Doris Meissner, the director of the US Immigration and Policy Program at the Migratory Policy Institute and INS commissioner in the Clinton administration, any initiatives for comprehensive immigration reform were pushed aside in this period because of the dramatic change in attitude following 9/11. "We've heard over and over again that the laws passed related to immigration since then are meant to protect national security, when the reality is they mainly have to do with immigration control," Meissner states.[8]

The data on this issue over the past decade support her view. A research project at Syracuse University called Transactional Records Access Clearinghouse (TRAC) analyzed millions of deportation cases over the decade following 9/11.[9] The results show that the number of deportees who were suspected terrorists or foreigners posing a danger to national security was *lower* in the decade after 9/11 than in the ten years leading up to it. But deportations of immigrants in general continued at a breakneck pace after the terror attacks. The data speak volumes: Cases of deportation specifically because of suspicion of terrorist activity were very rare before 9/11. In the prior decade, immigration courts processed 88 deportations on terrorism grounds. In the ten years after 9/11, only 37 cases were processed—fewer than half.

Another broader category for deportation is being a "threat to national security," which includes anyone who has ever belonged to the Communist or other totalitarian party, accused of sabotage or espionage, participated in Nazi persecutions or genocide, or would have a potentially seriously adverse effect on US foreign policy. In the ten years prior to 9/11, 384 people were deported on these grounds; in the decade after, the number was 360.

As far as deporting actual criminals, the figures are not much better. Under the Bush Administration and the first couple of years of the Obama government, the vast majority of deportees had no criminal records: 83.4 percent under Bush (2001–2009) and 82.8 percent under Obama (2009–2011).

And although in the initial phase of Obama's administration, the focus on deporting criminal offenders rose—18 percent more deportees had criminal records compared to President Bush's numbers—toward the end of his first term, that proportion dropped. For example, only 14.6 percent of all those deported in the first six months of 2011 had been convicted of a crime.

TRAC obtained this data by analyzing millions of deportation cases initiated by ICE, which had been in operation since 2003, and its predecessor, the INS. These deportations were carried out through the immigration courts, which are civil courts operating under the jurisdiction of the DOJ.

The records show that deportations carried out after 9/11 increased in terms of absolute numbers: from 1.6 million before 9/11, to 2.3 million after. But that increase is unrelated to any emphasis on foreigners who represented a threat to national security, terrorists or suspected terrorists, or dangerous criminals. Just the opposite, in fact: The number of deportations expedited for the express purpose of protecting the country from potentially violent acts actually diminished over the course of the decade following 9/11.

"What we are actually finding here is that the reality does not coincide with the discourse. The number of deportees for terrorism, national security, or for being criminals has dropped since 9/11. At the same time, deportations of undocumented immigrants with no ties to terrorism or any kind of criminal offense beyond immigration violations has risen," stated Sue Long, one of the researchers and a codirector of TRAC.[10]

"Terrorism" and "national security" are terms bureaucrats and politicians have used frequently following 9/11 to allude to the government's high priority in deporting and charging dangerous criminal foreigners.

The first director of ICE, Julie L. Myers, said in 2007, "I'm proud that we are entering our fifth year of service to the American people and our mission remains clear: to protect the United States and uphold public safety by targeting the people, money and materials that support terrorists and criminal activities."[11] The subsequent director of ICE, the secretaries of National Security, and President Obama himself have all made similar statements, which sound lofty and impressive but do not coincide with the facts.

The federal government has several grounds for initiating deportation: They include suspicion of terrorism or terrorist activity (including evidence of mere intent), criminal convictions, and, last—of lesser priority, according to public statements made by the Bush and Obama administrations—violations of immigration law.

The overriding concern over national security has itself become a fundamental part of the undocumented immigration problem, further straining a system unequipped to regulate and process the needed influx of workers and skilled professionals that the economy of the United States depends on.

The glaring absence of any sort of high-level, serious discussion on how to reform immigration law and best deal with immigrant workers, refugees, foreign students, and skilled professionals in a way that benefits the country is a result of how the nation responded to the threat of terrorism after 9/11. After that event, it was assumed that immigrants and foreigners were in and of themselves a great part of that threat. The events of 9/11 had an enormous impact on the country, and one of the areas most concretely affected has been immigration, with aggressive measures adopted to restrict or eliminate it altogether.

Anti-immigrant leanings, which have always existed, were revitalized and seemingly validated by the groundswell of fear about our vulnerable border and the threat of terrorism flooding across the Rio Grande in the Southern Border—even though, in fact, all of the terrorists involved in the 9/11 attacks arrived in the United States on airplanes and passed through customs with valid visas, not scrambling over the mountains of Arizona or hiking through the deserts of Texas.

SIX
"ILLEGALS" AND THE NEW HATE MOVEMENT

IN FEBRUARY 2011, SHAWNA FORDE BECAME THE SIXTY-SECOND WOMAN ON Death Row in the United States. A member of the border vigilante group the Minutemen, Forde was convicted in Tucson, Arizona, by a jury of eleven women and one man and sentenced to die by lethal injection. Her crime: the cold-blooded killing of nine-year-old Brisenia Flores and her father, Raul, in an incident in southern Arizona.

On May 30, 2009, there was a knock on the door of the trailer where the Flores family lived in Arivaca, a small town eleven miles north of the Mexican border. Two men and one woman claiming to be police officers demanded to be let in to search for a suspect.

Once inside, the intruders shot Raul to death, fired on his wife, Gina, and, as she pleaded for her life, fired two bullets in the nine-year-old girl's face. Gina testified in court that as she lay on the floor pretending to be dead, she heard her daughter begging them not to kill her. "I heard what happened," she said. "Brisenia asked them, Why did you shoot my dad? Why did you shoot my mom? Please, don't shoot me."[1]

But they did, killing Brisenia instantly. According to prosecutors, Forde had planned the attack to rob Raul Flores, believing he was a local narcotrafficker. She planned to take his money and drugs to finance the activities of her own paramilitary anti-immigrant group, formed after she was kicked out of the Minutemen.

Forde initially had joined the Minutemen, a group formed in 2005 in Arizona to patrol the border and prevent anyone from crossing into the United States illegally. Leaders of that organization have said that Forde was expelled because she was "unstable." So she formed her own militia group, the Minutemen American Defense. According to evidence presented in court, Forde believed that Raul "Junior" Flores was a major Mexican narcotrafficker. In actuality, Raul and his daughter were both American citizens born on US soil. There were no drugs in the trailer, or caches of cash, or any evidence of drug trafficking.

The double murder was deeply upsetting especially to the Latino community in Arizona and received widespread attention in the Spanish-language media. But the crime failed to capture the attention of the mainstream media, and scant coverage was devoted to it.

Just a few months later, however, another violent incident in southern Arizona did attract immediate and widespread attention in the state and across the country, becoming a flashpoint in the immigration debate: the murder of Robert Krentz, a rancher, in March 2010.

Krentz came from a well-known family who worked the land near Douglas, Arizona, for the past century. His body was found on March 27, 2010 in his all-terrain vehicle, along with his dog, who had also been killed. Krentz was well respected by the local community and had complained bitterly, as did other ranchers, of the damage unauthorized immigrants who crossed their property were doing to the land.

Over the past ten years, Arizona has become an increasingly critical point of entry for illegal drugs and undocumented immigrants crossing the border, and for good reason: The terrain is extremely dangerous, and precisely because of its mountains and deserts, extreme swings in temperature, and generally treacherous topography, it is not as well guarded as the border areas in California or parts of Texas.

One hundred fifty years ago, the Apache warrior Geronimo made good use of Arizona's mountain paths to evade the US cavalry. Today coyotes and narcotraffickers use the same routes to ferry migrants and drugs across the border. After Krentz was discovered dead from gunshot wounds, the media rushed to speculate that he could have been killed by an "illegal immigrant." The news story was quickly picked up nationwide and was echoed not just by other media outlets but by politicians as well, who demanded that the National Guard be sent to secure the border.

It was first speculated that Krentz had been killed by an "illegal immigrant" because he had radioed his brother shortly before his death and had used the word "illegal" to describe a man in apparent distress that he was helping. Then it was believed that he could have been killed by a drug "mule" (smuggler). Police dogs reportedly followed the killer's tracks for several miles in the direction of the Mexican border. The killer escaped back into Mexico, according to various reports.

There was no concrete evidence of who the killer was. In any case, Robert Krentz's murder caused an immediate outpouring of public grief and outrage, in contrast to the response to the shooting deaths of nine-year-old Brisenia and her father a few months earlier, which had elicited a muted response at most.

Legislators cited Krentz's death in debates over Arizona's SB 1070, to date the harshest anti-immigrant legislation ever considered by any state in the union. The proposed law, which would allow the police to detain anyone if there was a "reasonable suspicion" that they were undocumented, had been presented in the Arizona state legislature before Krentz was murdered, but the rancher's killing became the focal point of the debate. Some legislators even proposed (unsuccessfully) calling it the Robert Krentz law. On April 23, 2010, exactly one month after Krentz's death, Arizona's governor, Jan Brewer, signed SB 1070 into law, setting off a fervent national debate and several lawsuits.

As this book went to press, more than two years later, much of SB1070 still has not gone into effect. Given the US Supreme Court decision of June 2012, it most likely never will, with the exception of a narrow interpretation of the section that requires police to check the immigration status of people they have detained for other reasons. Much of SB1070 was struck down by the Supreme Court, and more legal challenges are forthcoming. Authorities have not been able to solve the mystery around the rancher's killing, although they did speculate that the killer may not have headed south and could be within the United States. One thing that has happened: Krentz's death shored up support among many Arizona residents for the state's radically anti-immigrant law.

In a strange twist of fate, the little discussed killing of little Brisenia and her father, Raul Flores, did find some justice in the court system. Robert Krentz's unsolved death pushed forward the country's most virulently anti-immigrant legislation ever passed by a state and spawned several copycat versions in other states.

THE MINUTEMAN PROJECT

Shawna Forde's supporters described her on their website as a "political prisoner" of the Department of Homeland Security and a victim of "racial profiling" because she is white. But Forde's activities in the border vigilante movement are well known.

According to Brian Levin, director of the Center for the Study of Hate and Extremism at the University of California in San Bernardino, Forde was "known within the anti-immigrant movement as an activist faithful to her cause, although others considered her a lunatic who could lose her mind at any moment."[2]

What is indisputable is that at the time of the killing, Forde had an ideological obsession: She was fervently anti-immigrant. And she was not alone. Although acts of extreme violence like the killings committed by Forde are the exception, vigilante groups serving as a wellspring of hate did not operate in a vacuum but within a broader political and media context that support the notion that there is no control at all over the borders and that undocumented immigrants are destroying the country.

On one hand, some politicians latched onto the immigration issue to exploit voters' fears about a supposed "illegal alien invasion" and pick up some easy votes. And on the other, the Minutemen "patrolled" the border, with the explicit support of high-profile politicians, such as California's former governor Arnold Schwarzenegger, himself an immigrant from Austria who came to the country legally. During his 2005 reelection campaign, Schwarzenegger had the inspired idea to praise the vigilante group's activities in a radio interview.

Although at the time President George W. Bush had condemned the Minutemen, referring to them as "vigilantes" operating outside of the law, Schwarzenegger did not hesitate to use the group's activities to ingratiate himself with his state's Republican base. A large number of Republicans openly sympathized with the group and responded positively to the governor's anti-immigrant rhetoric.

"I think they've done a terrific job," Schwarzenegger told listeners of the *John and Ken Show* on conservative radio station KFI in Los Angeles, one of many radio and television shows that spends a good part of its airtime blaming immigrants for all manner of local and national problems. The governor went on: "They've cut down the crossing of illegal immigrants a huge percentage. It just shows that it works when you go and make an effort. . . . It's just that our federal government is not doing their job."[3]

The Minuteman Project, when it was born in October 2004, aimed to be a group of renegade vigilantes and adopted the historic moniker of the Minuteman militias that fought against the British army in the Revolutionary War.

The twenty-first-century Minutemen were not as successful as their namesakes. The group was comprised mostly of activists on the outer fringes of the immigration debate; their main objective was to organize ordinary citizens to patrol the borders, stop the flow of illegal immigrants, and defend the homeland. The Minutemen offered to assist the official US Border Patrol by reporting suspected illegal immigrants whom they saw crossing the border and setting up makeshift guard posts. There is no evidence that the Border Patrol collaborated or acted on their tips, and later there were even reports that the US Border Patrol leadership told its agents not to give any special attention to Minutemen calls. But the symbolism of the group's actions turned out to be very attractive to the news media, and they were widely reported on, vaulting them to national prominence and prompting President Bush's characterization of group members as vigilantes.

"I'm against vigilantes in the United States of America," Bush declared in a March 2005 speech during a continental summit held in Texas with Mexican president Vicente Fox and Canadian prime minister Paul Martin. He added, "I'm for enforcing the law in a rational way."[4]

The ad hoc border patrols received a great deal of coverage in the media in the summer of 2005, just as Congress was debating various pieces of proposed immigration legislation. The Minutemen claimed to have tens of thousands of members, but generally their patrol groups consisted of dozens or, occasionally, hundreds of people.

According to press reports at the time and a chapter of the book *Global Vigilantes* by University of California at Irvine's professor Leo R. Chavez, the goal of the Minuteman Project's founder, Jim Gilchrist, was to pressure the Bush administration to tighten security at the border.[5] In spite of Bush's condemnation of his organization, Gilchrist met his goal.

A veteran of the Vietnam War, retired accountant, and resident of Orange County, California, Jim Gilchrist founded the Minuteman Project with Chris Simcox, a troubled former Los Angeles school teacher with a criminal record. Just a year earlier, Simcox had been convicted of carrying a semiautomatic pistol within national park grounds, lying about it, and giving a false report to police.

Both men subsequently tried to start political careers, ambitions that no doubt accounted for at least a part of their motivations for launching the Minuteman Project. In 2005, Gilchrist ran for US Congress as an independent, representing California's 48th District, and Simcox challenged Senator John McCain in the Republican Party's primary in 2010 in Arizona. Both men lost by wide margins.

But in the spring of 2005, the angels seemed to be on their side. Well mannered and looking like a business executive, Gilchrist came across as a moderate, rational person, an image in stark contrast to his extreme anti-immigrant views. He became the movement's intellectual leader, giving interviews to anyone who asked, including the Hispanic media, explaining that the goals of the Minuteman patrols had already been reached even before they began.

"This thing was a dog and pony show designed to bring in the media and get the message out, and it worked," Gilchrist said during one of the hundreds of interviews he gave, talking about the "thousands of activists" he had mobilized."[6] (In the spring of 2005, the number never surpassed two hundred.) President Bush announced in March of that year that five hundred new Border Patrol agents would be sent to the Arizona–Mexico border and would be reinforced with planes. His announcement came just two days before the first Minuteman patrol set out on April 1, and of course Gilchrist claimed victory: "None of this would have happened if it wasn't for the Minuteman action."[7]

The national media was all too eager to cover Gilchrist's movement, with ample coverage on Fox News, the *Lou Dobbs* show on CNN, and many others. Practically all the major news outlets reported on the "movement" in one way or another; coverage was so great that reporters and news trucks often outnumbered the activists they were covering.

Not even Gilchrist himself stayed at the desolate stretch of border in Arizona for the entire month of April. He declared victory in the middle of the month and left to pursue other activities, including his run for Congress. The numbers of undocumented immigrants crossing the border did decline during the height of the Minuteman Project's actions. Gilchrist attributed this solely to the Minutemen themselves; others suggested that the legions of reporters, media trucks, and stories in the press on both sides of the border had more to do with it. Gilchrist and Simcox, both men with outsize egos and leadership aspirations, quickly parted ways, and the group was split in two: the Minuteman Project and Simcox's new splinter group, the Minuteman Civil Defense Corps (MCDC). Although they received less media attention, both groups continued operating as nonprofits, accepting donations, vowing to support like-minded political candidates, and even planning on erecting their own border fences.

Both organizations eventually were plagued by accusations of misuse of funds and fraught with internal power struggles and conflicts. The more scrutinized of the two groups turned out to be Simcox's MCDC. Simcox joined forces with high-profile African American Republican Alan Keyes and various fundamentalist Christian groups that he supported with donations and resources to promote political candidates with a similar agenda. Together they formed an umbrella group called the Secure Borders Coalition. At first glance, it's hard to see what Simcox's group, an African American conservative, and extremist groups of fundamentalists could have in common, but apparently they had no trouble finding overlapping interests.

The Secure Borders Coalition accepted millions of dollars in donations from private citizens who believed in the group's objectives, one of which was to construct a high-tech wall similar to one in Israel at a cost of $150 per foot. The funds seem to have disappeared into thin air, however, along with plans for the wall, which ended up being a few miles of rudimentary fencing similar to what ranchers use to keep their animals in.

Reports on mismanagement of funds came not only from MCDC critics but from well-known and respected conservative media outlets, such as the *Washington Times,* which in 2006 published an extensive article describing concerns the group's own followers had about a lack of transparency and how its leaders were managing donations.

Ultimately, the effectiveness of the Minuteman movement as a whole is highly questionable, and it never again attracted the sort of frenzied media attention it received in 2005. Gilchrist's group, re-formed under the name the Minuteman Project Inc., still exists, although various internal disputes led to lawsuits, and the former public accountant temporarily severed ties with the organization he had founded.

After several lawsuits and countersuits, Gilchrist regained control of the group in 2007. The homepage of its website reads: "A multi-ethnic immigration law enforcement advocacy group. Operating within the law to support enforcement of the law"[8]— much more humble objectives than Gilchrist had at the beginning, when he sought to use citizen militias to perform the work that the government refused to do.

Gilchrist eventually came to say publicly that the movement had been diluted by the successive divisions and the formation of offshoot groups that were not faithful to the original group's objectives.[9] He emphatically claimed to have no association at all with Shawna Forde's faction, and he tried to put forth an image of operating "within the law."

As for Simcox, his group, the MCDC, shut down for good in March 2010, a year after he left it to pursue a run for the Senate against Republican incumbent John McCain. The MCDC's membership rolls steadily dwindled, and by the time it formally ceased operations, it was no longer conducting patrols along the border in Arizona, Texas, and New Mexico.

One offshoot group called the Minuteman Corps of California has managed to hang on. Its main area of operation, dubbed Camp Vigilance, is an eight-acre campground located on private property in Vista, California, two and a half miles from the border. On its website (http://www.minutemancorpsca.com), the group's administrators invite everyday citizens to patrol the border and camp at the site. Photos show recreational vehicles on a snowy day parked at the high-elevation camp, smiling people enjoying a casual open-air buffet meal under a tent, and lots of red, white, and blue. It's a social club with a common purpose: fighting undocumented immigration.

A LEGACY OF HATE

Over time, splinter groups and factions descending from the original Minuteman Project led to the formation of various smaller organizations incorporating ideologies of the Patriot movement that had emerged in the 1990s. Such ideology was fueled by conspiracy theories, including the belief that the influx of illegal immigrants is all part of a plan by the Mexican government to "reconquer" the Southwest. In its report "The Second Wave: The Return of the Militias," the Southern Poverty Law Center discusses the resurgence in recent years of patriotic militia groups who originally inspired the deadliest domestic terrorist attack in the nation's history: the 1995 bombing of Oklahoma City's federal building, in which 168 people were killed.[10]

But although in the 1990s militias tended to emphasize fighting the government and refusing to pay taxes on ideological grounds, the new militias have more explicit racial overtones: they were formed in the late 2000s as a reaction to the election of a half-black, half-white man to the presidency and to the growth of the Latino population throughout the country. This fusion and overlap of racist groups and "patriotic" libertarian militias has become more commonplace in recent years. Even back in 2003, before the Minuteman Project existed, and before the most recent debates on possible immigration reform measures took place in Congress, the Anti-Defamation League (ADL) warned of the dangerous alliance between white supremacists and anti-immigrant groups.

"Anti-immigration groups are engaged in a campaign of vigilantism and intimidation, and their ideology has all the hallmarks of the hateful rhetoric promoted by anti-Semites and racists," Bill Straus, the ADL's regional director in Arizona, declared in 2003, just as the first vigilante militias began to operate along the border. Straus added, "We are greatly concerned that the collusion of anti-immigration groups and their extremist sympathizers is contributing to the growing climate of intolerance, lawlessness and violence along the Arizona–Mexico border."[11]

In the days and weeks after the Minuteman Project was founded, sporadic reports described white supremacist groups aligning themselves with the Minutemen or forming new groups emphasizing an anti-immigrant message.

Although the existence of these marginal extremist groups was certainly troublesome, they themselves did not grow to represent anything greater than very small group of radicals. But gradually, and thanks to their use of media and ties to Washington lobbying groups, they have come to exercise greater influence on society as a whole. This influence grew as worries about the United States becoming a "Third World" country and demographic changes—what racist groups called "the invasion"—became a routine topic of conversation, along with immigration, thanks to local and national radio and television shows. They also received the backing of, by all outward appearances, respectable nonprofit groups headquartered in Washington advocating for stricter immigration controls. Hate crimes perpetrated against Latinos slowly but steadily increased in number over the course of the first decade of the twenty-first century, according to Federal Bureau of Investigation (FBI) statistics, which themselves never tell the whole story but offer only a glimpse of the tip of the iceberg because many manifestations of hate, including crimes and speech, are not reported to the authorities.[12]

In addition to various high-profile cases of hate crimes that took place across the country, the consequences of rising anti-immigrant sentiment were seen in political movements in cities and states designed to legislate a virtual ever-tightening noose for undocumented immigrants from which there is no escape.

A HATE CRIME

In a column published in Los Angeles Spanish-language newspaper *La Opinión* on May 5, 2009, I wrote just one story of many that could have been reported:

> He was a young undocumented Mexican, twenty-five years old. His name was Luis Eduardo Ramirez Zavala, a father of two. On July 12, 2008 he was surrounded by six teenagers, high-school football players from Shenandoah, in Pennsylvania, as he walked his fiancée Crystal's little sister home.
>
> There were insults, there was a fight. Luis Eduardo died, his skull shattered.

Before and during the trial, witnesses reported that they heard some of the young attackers shouting "go back to Mexico" and other things too vile to be printed.

After the killing, local authorities began making excuses for the boys, one of whom was a relative of a local law enforcement officer. The case rose to national prominence, thanks to Latino and other activist groups who protested, and formal charges were brought against two of the attackers, Brandon Piekarsky and Derrick Donchak. The prosecution presented several witnesses who testified to the particularly violent nature of the assault on Ramirez; the defense did not put either defendant on the stand.

At the end of the criminal trial in May 2009, after deliberating for nearly eight hours, the all-white jury found the two young men guilty of assault and other lesser charges but not guilty of homicide or ethnic intimidation.

Gladys Limon, an attorney for the Mexican American Legal Defense and Education Fund, an organization that provided legal assistance in the case, stated that she could not understand the jury's decision, unless the jurors did not understand the law or the judge's instructions.

"Irrefutable evidence was presented at the trial about a meeting which took place at the home of one of the young men involved, with local law enforcement, where they all decided what their stories would be. And the defendants were acquitted of lesser charges which clearly warranted convictions, such as endangering the life of another person," Limon asserted. "What we have here is a total collapse of the criminal justice system."[13]

It's interesting to read stories published in the local press. Thirty-six-year-old John Dombrosky, a resident of Shenandoah and the attackers' football coach, said that they were "good boys who had had too much to drink and got in a fight . . . unfortunately, someone died. Boys fight. I feel sorry for the children—the Mexican's kids—but he threw some punches too."

The young Mexican man threw some punches to defend himself against six football players, fell down, smashed his skull, and then somehow kicked himself in the head, killing himself.

Other residents had a more clear-eyed view. "If it had been the other way around, they would have hanged them," said Noreen Bayliff, who lives in Shenandoah. "That man died, no matter what his immigration status was. There are problems between whites and Hispanics here. This town was built by Irish, Italian, and Eastern European immigrants, and there has always been a lot of prejudice."[14]

One month after a verdict was reached in the criminal trial in Shenandoah, a federal grand jury indicted Brandon Piekarsky and Derrick Donchak on hate crime charges and three police officers involved in the alleged cover-up of the case.

A Pennsylvania jury found Piekarsky and Donchak guilty of a hate crime resulting in a death and sentenced them to nine years in prison. A month earlier, the former chief of police, Matthew Nestor, had been found guilty of falsifying a police report, and the police officer, William Moyer, had been convicted of lying to the FBI, while another officer was acquitted.

Luis Ramirez was killed due to a hatred of immigrants.

SEVEN

STATES TAKE THE LAW INTO THEIR OWN HANDS

THE NAME OF THE TOWN IN THE MOJAVE DESERT IS HARD TO PRONOUNCE: Pahrump. Located in Nevada about forty-five miles northeast of Las Vegas, it's very close to the California state line. The name "Pahrump" comes from a Native American word meaning "rock water," a reference to the underground natural wells under the valley. For many years, the only people who lived near Pahrump were a few ranchers. After 1960, when the first paved road was constructed, it became a sort of rest stop between Death Valley and Las Vegas and started to grow.

The little town of Pahrump gained a measure of notoriety in 2008 when the King of Pop himself, Michael Jackson, built a studio there after he was cleared of charges of child molestation. He was performing in Las Vegas, and cameramen and paparazzi became a regular presence near his desert enclave.

But that wasn't Pahrump's first time in the spotlight: In 2006, in a three-to-two vote, the city council attracted attention from around the globe when it passed an ordinance prohibiting residents from flying any foreign country's flag unless an American flag was flown above it.

As absurd as it sounds—not to mention unconstitutional, since flying a flag is an act of free expression protected by the

First Amendment—many residents of the town with the funny name agreed with their leaders when the measure was passed on November 14, 2006. It also included provisions to make English the town's official language and to bar undocumented immigrants from receiving any kind of social services—services that, according to the *Las Vegas Review Journal,* could not legally be denied, such as education, emergency medical attention, or use of a public library.

What was going on in Pahrump?

An incident that occurred shortly after the ordinance was passed can provide some insight. Offended by the measure, local residents Bob and Liese Tamburrino decided to engage in a little civil disobedience and hung Polish and Italian flags over their home's garage.

The next day, they found the Italian flag had been pelted with raw eggs in the night. Bob Tamburrino drew his own conclusion: "They must have thought it was a Mexican flag," he said, since the Italian and Mexican flags are the same colors, but the Mexican one has a shield in the middle.

What was going on in Pahrump was also happening in other small towns and cities in far-flung areas around the country. The presence of foreigners, especially Mexicans, came as something of a shock to longtime local residents who hadn't seen any drastic changes in their population over the last several decades. And these newcomers spoke another language and had dark skin.

Stories from local newspapers provide more context. The initial proposal to ban the display of stand-alone foreign flags was initiated by council member Michael Miraglia, who declared flatly to the press, "I'm sick of people not speaking English." To illustrate his point, he mentioned a recent experience in a restaurant when a worker had not understood when he had asked for a napkin.

Welcome to the twenty-first century, when states and municipalities are passing laws that are very difficult, if not impossible, to enforce and often are unconstitutional. What these laws do accomplish is they make people feel better about what's made them so uncomfortable: the rapid increase in the number of foreigners in their midst. And sponsoring these measures is a quick and easy way for local politicians with larger ambitions to make a name for themselves.

The general reasoning behind all of the restrictive initiatives seems to be plausible. The basic argument looks serious on its face: The rapid influx of undocumented people threatens public safety, raises costs for local government, and is simply intolerable because the newcomers are breaking the law. And, supporters assert the "illegals" take jobs away from American citizens.

The real problem with the implementation of these measures is that their effects are dubious and the motives behind them are even more questionable. It isn't clear what benefit to the community is achieved by banning a flag or the use of all languages besides English, or denying social services that do not even exist in a particular community or that can't be legally taken away from undocumented people. Nor is there much evidence that the end goal—the outright expulsion of all foreigners from the community—is being achieved as a result. Demographers have repeatedly shown that Mexicans leave a town only when they are not able to find work, the reason they left Mexico in the first place; then they relocate to other areas where there is work to be had and start building a new community there.

In Pahrump, some immigrants did move away, frightened by all the media attention and the measures passed meant to harass them.[1] The same thing happened in Hazleton, Pennsylvania, discussed in the next chapter. But within just a few years, in both places, the growth of the Latino population continues unabated, as shown by figures from the 2010 census.[2]

The sharp increase in population has been deeply unsettling to many locals. Pahrump only had 2,000 residents in 1980, but that number had more than tripled to 7,000 by 1990, and more than tripled again by 2000 to a population of 24,000. The 2010 census reported 36,000 residents in Pahrump, eighteen times the number three decades earlier. But in 2000, the minority population was still small, and census workers reported they were surprised by the lack of children in the town. At the time, the Hispanic population represented 7.6 percent of the total, while "non-Hispanic whites" comprised 91 percent. African Americans were only 2 percent of the total.

Over the next decade, the growth of Las Vegas and its housing market resulted in abundant job opportunities in the construction and hospitality industries, attracting a new population of workers. By 2009, the white population of Pahrump as a percentage of the total had declined sharply for the first time, to 74 percent, while Hispanics reached 15 percent and African Americans reached 12 percent.

More and more businesses catering to the immigrant community began popping up around town, with signs in Spanish, and hearing people speaking it in the streets and in the schools became more commonplace. No apparent rise in crime was reported.

What happened in that little town in the desert is playing out in cities and towns all across the United States. Twenty years ago, the immigrant population from Mexico and other Latin American countries was largely concentrated in states that already had an established Hispanic population, such as California, New York, Florida, and Texas. The situation changed very fast in the decade starting in 2000.

"Latino immigrants have been spreading out across the United States in search of jobs that are no longer as plentiful in the states where there is already a large immigrant population," observes Gary Painter, an economist at the University of Southern California studying the effects immigrants have on the economy. "Especially over the last decade they have gone to places where people are not used to seeing many Hispanics, like Kansas, Wyoming, and Washington state."[3]

This phenomenon relates directly to the surge in local statutes aiming to control immigration. Demographic and sociological studies show that the cities and counties that have passed measures against immigrants without legal status over the last decade all experienced a dramatic increase in the number of residents from other countries in that same time frame.

"The data shows that changes in the proportion of the foreign population between 1990 and 2000 can predict where local legislative initiatives will appear, just as unemployment rates and the highest proportion of foreigners can," points out Kevin O'Neil, a researcher at Princeton University's Demographics Department.[4]

In other words, the influx of people who speak another language and look different generates fear in the established local population, and they react based on those fears. Virtually none of the communities that have attempted to rid themselves of immigrants through local legislation considered the positive impact newer arrivals may have on the economy or the fact that some immigrants relocating from other states may be bona fide US citizens, even if they do speak another language.

In Pahrump, the simple presence of a largely Mexican immigrant community generated palpable discomfort. At the city council meeting held to discuss the issue, dozens of local residents attended to voice their concerns. Elliott Brainard's comment summed up the general mood: "These people don't speak English, they use up money and resources that our citizens need," he said. Another man with a stars-and-stripes bandanna tied around his head wore a T-shirt that read "Speak English or get the fuck out."[5]

Most of the other people who spoke at the meeting voiced the same opinion. Those who tried to argue in favor of tolerance or against the legislative initiative were shouted down. Several citizens of Mexican origin who operated local businesses reported having been harassed by others in the town.

Lucero Enriquez, the owner of Mi Ranchito Market in Pahrump, told a reporter with the *Las Vegas Review Journal* that she had received an anonymous postcard in the mail that said, "It makes us sick to see Mexicans with 2 or 3 kids and the mother's pregnant with twins walking around our streets . . . you are abusing and destroying our welfare system."[6]

And so the story goes. The little city in Nevada was not the only place where this drama played out in the first decade of the twenty-first century, although few legislative measures were as futile and difficult to enforce as Pahrump's banning of foreign flags.

Between 2000 and 2010, more than two hundred municipalities across the country adopted or considered adopting measures meant to curb immigration, ranging from prohibiting renting housing to undocumented immigrants, to requiring local police to collaborate with federal immigration authorities, to establishing "English Only" statutes. Another popular initiative focused on closing down "day worker centers" set up by local governments to coordinate hiring workers who would otherwise gather on street corners or in parking lots, waiting for someone to offer them a job for the day in construction, gardening, and other types of labor.

More recently, calls for sidestepping the whole political process and solving the problem the old-fashioned way, with a gun, have become more common. Oddly, the most extreme commentaries have come from politicians in districts where the presence of immigrants is a very new phenomenon, such as State Representative Virgil Peck, from the heartland plains of Kansas, a state that saw the Latino population expand by 59 percent between 2000 and 2010.

"Looks like to me, if shooting these immigrating feral hogs works, maybe we have found a solution to our illegal immigration problem," he said in early 2011. His remarks were widely broadcast, and his colleagues pressured him to retract the statement. The state congressman apologized without apologizing, saying "I was just speaking like a person from southeast Kansas."[7]

The intentions behind the movement for immigrant-free zones are becoming clearer. In the summer of 2011, Loren Nichols, a candidate for city council in Kennewick, Washington, said that if he was elected, he would enact a measure forcing all "illegals" to get out of town within thirty days.

"And they'd be lucky to get that much time," said Nichols, a fifty-five-year-old navy veteran who considers illegal immigration "the rape of my country." "And if they don't get out, they'll face the consequences."[8]

Nichols added that he supports the death penalty for illegal immigrants, in the style of the Old West. "I think they should be shot when they cross the border," he asserted, straight-faced.

All of these theatrical displays show how emotional the issue of immigration has become. These proposals do not provide meaningful solutions, and many are very difficult or impossible to enforce. But they do attract supporters among those who are already predisposed to blame immigrants for society's ills, real or imagined.

In the end, all the legislative efforts in Pahrump did not amount to much. The immigrants did not leave, and the ordinance banning foreign flags never took effect. The town's sheriff refused to enforce it; he had enough actual work to do fighting real crimes. New local politicians came on the scene and turned their attention to more pressing matters.

Any substantive discussion about the real effects of illegal immigration or immigration in general—positive, negative, or some combination of the two—tends to be pushed aside, and conclusions are drawn based on superficial politics. What has been extensively discussed is the negative effects of these local ordinances.

And although a significant number of municipalities enacted local ordinances targeting immigrants, at least seventy cities and states around the country have enacted regulations explicitly separating fighting crime from immigration. In Los Angeles, this separation is widely accepted and has been in place for some time because there is a belief that wherever local police are required to go after undocumented immigrants simply because they are undocumented, public safety suffers because those immigrants naturally avoid cooperating with the police on any matter.

That's the conclusion the leaders of the city of Los Angeles reached back in 1979. Even the chief of police at the time, Daryl Gates, agreed, and he was hardly a "soft," pro-immigrant liberal. Gates had a reputation as being very hard-line, openly mocking civil rights groups. His police department was widely viewed as out of control and plagued by racism. These issues boiled over in the 1992 race riots, laying bare the racial and social fault lines in the city and the contempt his officers inspired in minority communities.

Gates agreed that allowing local police officers to act as agents of the federal government and demanding to see immigrants' papers would serve only to isolate and alienate the Latino community, causing them to avoid all communication with the police and refuse to serve as witnesses. They would not help in any crime-fighting efforts for fear of being deported.

Until that time, an L.A. police officer could detain anyone at all and ask to see their documentation. With the implementation of Special Order 40 in 1979 as official LAPD policy, the police can ask to see immigration documentation only if a credible reason exists to suspect the person had committed a crime. The measure continues to be actively observed in Los Angeles more than three decades later, and with good reason.

The most important police associations and law enforcement agencies in the United States have reaffirmed the notion that the same officers should not enforce general criminal law and immigration law. The National Association of Police Chiefs authored a report in 2004 that explained the reasoning behind this approach. "Local police departments depend on the collaboration of immigrants, legal and illegal, to solve all kinds of crimes and threats to public order."

In just a few years, the movement to strengthen laws against undocumented immigrants at all levels had spread across the country and become a part of national politics: Hundreds of localities and at least half of the fifty states had considered enacting restrictive laws against immigrants.

Alabama, Arizona, Georgia, and Oklahoma passed laws granting—and even requiring—local and state police the authority to detain any person they suspected of being undocumented; they established punitive measures against anyone who transported, offered work, rented apartments, or even gave a ride to an undocumented immigrant. Except for some sections relating to hiring undocumented workers, the larger part of these laws have been overturned in federal courts or suspended pending final decisions from judges at all levels of the justice system.

But in early 2011, thanks to the negative economic and sociological effects of the most famous anti-immigrant legislation passed to date, the Arizona Law, its copycats in Georgia and Alabama and the impact on the agricultural economics in those states (which is discussed in detail in Chapter 9), proposed similar legislative initiatives have met with negative reactions. In Arizona, the business community strenuously protested SB 1070 and succeeded in blocking other even more restrictive measures proposed in the legislature.

As long as broader national and uniform legislation addressing immigration is not enacted, and as long as there is no substantial improvement in the economy, most experts agree it is unlikely that the balance will shift in favor of more moderate immigration policies any time soon. Politically, like so many other times in our nation's history, the United States debates internally about its future and the sustainability of its founding principles as a nation of immigrants that remains the land of opportunity for those with the need and the courage to make it. It remains to be seen if those principles will survive into the new millennium.

EIGHT
HAZLETON, PENNSYLVANIA
A COMMUNITY'S DEMOGRAPHIC SHOCK

OUR STORY OPENS IN THE FOOTHILLS OF PENNSYLVANIA, IN A SMALL CITY whose name was misspelled at its founding in the 1800s: With the stroke of a pen, "Hazelton" became Hazleton. And that's how it appeared splashed across the headlines at the dawn of the twenty-first century, when the municipality passed an avalanche of local laws intended to banish immigrants from within its borders.

In 2006, Mayor Lou Barletta, a descendant of the Italian immigrants who had settled in the area generations ago to work in the coal mines, spearheaded a movement to resolve the supposed "illegal immigrant crime wave" plaguing his city. His plan: pass a local law that would punish anyone who rented apartments to undocumented immigrants and anyone who employed them. He also intended to make English Hazleton's "official language." Businesses catering to Latinos with signs in Spanish had become commonplace in the small city, and the language could be heard spoken in the streets, just as in many other communities across the United States.

To Barletta, undocumented immigrants had become a serious problem: They were to blame for crime, drugs, and an overall lack of security in the town. To illustrate his point, Barletta told a story of several "illegals" approaching a neighbor and killing him with a gunshot to the head. One of the attackers had four different IDs. The mayor's statements were printed in the *Washington Post,* which published a profile piece about what was going on in the Pennsylvania city.[1] That article also pointed out that very few crimes actually had been committed by undocumented immigrants in Hazleton in recent years.

"To the illegals, I would recommend you leave," Barletta said in mid-2006 when the municipal council voted four to one in favor of the ordinance at a lively meeting. With a flair for the dramatic, the mayor had arrived at the council meeting wearing a bulletproof vest, to protect himself from "illegals."

The approval of the measure catapulted Hazleton onto the national stage, and Barletta was suddenly a sought-after guest on national talk shows and news shows, such as Lou Dobbs on CNN. Dobbs, who began his career as a financial journalist, was in the crosshairs of several activist groups for his birther theories, espousing that President Obama had not been born in the United States, and because the content of his show every afternoon on one of the best-known news networks in the world had become nothing more than a constant litany of extremist anti-immigrant rhetoric. (Dobbs's show was abruptly canceled in November 2009 with no explanation.)

What had happened in Hazleton that made it such fertile ground for an anti-immigrant movement?

In fact, it was one tragic event that unleashed the fury of the mayor and many of the town's residents, according to David Sosar, a lifelong resident of Hazleton and professor at Kings College in neighboring Wilkes-Barre, Pennsylvania.

"There were a few incidents, the best known of which was the shooting death of a young man on Green Street in 2006, half a block from the local paper's office. Green Street intersects with Wyoming, one of the streets with lots of immigrants; there were many stores and businesses there established by that population, who came from New York and New Jersey," Sosar observed.[2]

Among those arrested for the crime were two undocumented Dominican men and this was the straw that broke the camel's back, resulting in the passage of the anti-immigrant ordinance, even though charges were eventually dropped by the district attorney because of a lack of evidence.

Barletta also argued that "illegals" financially burdened the local government, which had to pay for security, education, and other costs; in fact, most of those costs were covered by the state or the federal government. He never discussed how the local community benefited from immigrant labor and had revitalized a town that had been in a severe decline at the beginning of the decade.

"It wouldn't be the first or the last time that a crime that shook a community was used to push through draconian laws," observed José Pérez, a lawyer with the Puerto Rican Legal Defense Fund, which filed a lawsuit challenging Hazleton's anti-immigrant ordinance. "They did it in Arizona with a rancher's murder, which the media initially attributed to an 'illegal' only to later back off that theory, and it's been done with other cases. The reality is in the legal challenge when the lawyers took his testimony, Mayor Barletta could not come up with any proof that the presence of immigrants was contributing to higher crime rates, nor could he prove any of his other theories."

Whenever the suspects in robberies or drug-related crimes were Hispanic, the authorities and local newspaper tended to emphasize their legal status, reinforcing the idea that undocumented immigrants in general were criminals.

For example, an article published in the local *Times Leader* described a police action on September 7, 2007, called Operation Boomerang, which involved a hundred local, state, and federal agents and targeted a local cocaine ring in Hazleton. Between fifteen and twenty suspects were taken into custody that day, and more arrests were expected to follow. Only two of the suspects were undocumented immigrants, but that fact was highlighted in the article's subheading. The piece also described the arrest of Louis "Jose" Gonzalez, who had several aliases and "an FBI file dating back to 1984 with arrests in San Juan, Puerto Rico, on auto theft charges, and in New York City on marijuana sale charges."[3]

It's not clear whether Gonzalez was one of the two "illegals" or whether he was Puerto Rican or Dominican. If he was Puerto Rican, he would be Hispanic but not "illegal," since all Puerto Ricans are citizens of the United States, a fact that apparently still escapes many.

Never one to pass up an opportunity to highlight the illegal immigrant problem, Mayor Barletta proclaimed, "All the narcotraffickers, drug users, illegals and gang members who were lucky enough not to have gotten caught this time should ask themselves, who will be next? It could be you."[4]

His unedited remarks were printed in a local paper. The mayor and the local media constantly referred to the hundreds of immigrants who were most likely undocumented and living in Hazleton, who had businesses and families, and except for not having valid immigration papers were entirely law-abiding in the same breath as the very worst criminal elements. Yet the criminals who were also undocumented immigrants accounted for just a very tiny fraction of the hundreds and perhaps thousands of Latinos who had come to the area in recent years in search of a better life.

It was a potentially explosive situation for a long-established working-class town like Hazleton. A profound demographic shift had taken place there in the previous few years, a change that for the first time was playing out in small cities and towns far removed from the major urban centers throughout the country.

These small towns had been relatively untouched by the large influx of Latinos coming to the big cities in the 1980s and 1990s.

In 2000, Hazleton had approximately twenty thousand residents. Of those, fewer than 5 percent were of Hispanic origin, mostly Dominicans and Puerto Ricans who had left the high cost of living and stress levels of New York City and the greater metropolitan area.

Like many small towns, Hazleton had enjoyed a sort of golden age in past centuries but had to fight to survive in the twentieth century and was undeniably in decline by the 1980s. Abundant coal deposits had been discovered there in the nineteenth century, and the local coal mines helped to solidify the primacy of US industry on the global stage. But by World War II, the coal mining industry had waned, as the mines were depleted and relatively cleaner forms of energy were developed and exploited.

The local economy was next revitalized by the textile industry, with the production of natural and synthetic fabrics for clothing manufacturers. The Duplan Silk Corporation, a major textile manufacturer of silk and nylon, had its largest mill in Hazleton in the first half of the twentieth century, finally closing its doors in 1953. It was rumored locally that the Italian mafia was using the town and its textile industry as a front for illegal activities.

But by the close of the twentieth century, Hazleton was on a downward path, with a desolate downtown abandoned by many of the national chains and a struggling economy. In 2002, US News & World Report published an article titled "A Town in Need of a Tomorrow: Letter from Pennsylvania," describing the problems of the once-prosperous town, which, in its heyday, had been the third in the country to have electricity.[5]

By the middle of the decade, things had changed: According to the census, Hazleton officially had five thousand Latino residents, a full quarter of its population.

The discomfort with different ethnic or cultural groups was nothing new in that corner of Pennsylvania, according to David Sosar. "I'm a descendant of Italians and Poles, and in these small towns, there are still some people who make ethnic jokes. When they're uncomfortable they'll make racial references or use insults. That's how it is in these small towns, it's always been that way," he observes.

But this time, changes in the local population's demographics came about extremely fast. Reports on out-of-control "illegals" were too much for the town, and residents of Hazleton, including some immigrants themselves, commented that crime did seem to be rising. Barletta's histrionics and political gamesmanship did the rest.

The mayor always spoke about rising crime rates in the most general terms—crimes that were, according to him, mostly perpetrated by illegal immigrants. Barletta told the *Washington Post* that "illegals" were committing more and more violent crimes, with more drug dealers being arrested.[6] He never cited actual numbers.

The newspapers did not give the same attention to how newcomers arriving from other cities, including Latino immigrants, were revitalizing Hazleton by buying old homes and fixing them up; opening small businesses, such as convenience stores, restaurants, and barbershops; and providing much-needed labor to local factories, especially meat and poultry processing plants.

Barletta had his sights set on Washington, where Congress was in the middle of debates on immigration reform and what to do about undocumented immigrants in general. Meanwhile in April and May 2006, tens of thousands of immigrants and their supporters took to the streets in rallies and marches in cities across the country, demanding the legalization of millions of undocumented immigrants and protesting attempts by Congress to further criminalize them. Those very immigrants took part in the marches, fearlessly exposing their status. Some rallies were sharply criticized for displaying foreign flags. In the end, the massive protests generated political debate and inspired fear in some sectors, goading local governments to work harder to come up with their own solutions, or at least start talking about the inadequacy of the current immigration system. How dare those "illegals" demand anything at all?

A politician with outsize ambitions, Barletta could sense which way the political winds were blowing. He had been the mayor of his hometown of Hazleton since 1999, after an unsuccessful attempt to become a professional baseball player and stints working in his family's construction and heating oil businesses. He had also launched his own pavement marking business, which became so successful that by the time he sold it in 2000 it was the largest company of its kind in Pennsylvania.

Barely three years after he was elected mayor, in 2002, Barletta ran for Congress for the first time and was defeated. He lost again when he ran in 2008, a generally unfavorable year for Republican candidates, with particular challenges for Barletta, who had courted the largely Democratic constituency of Hazleton to win the mayor's office. He won reelection as mayor in 2003 and 2007 and finally achieved his dream of a seat in the nation's Congress in 2010 representing Pennsylvania's 11th District, the year the Republicans took back the majority of the seats in the House of Representatives.

When Barletta left Hazleton for the capital in 2010, not much had changed in his hometown. The American Civil Liberties Union and the Puerto Rican Legal Defense Fund had sued Hazleton in 2006 over its anti-immigrant ordinance and obtained a court order blocking its application while its constitutionality was debated. The legal battle went on. In the short term, the town did see a noticeable exodus of immigrants frightened by the attention and hostility toward all Latinos that the law had inspired—how would law enforcement determine who was legal and who was not?

But there is still a significant Hispanic community in Hazleton, and even though the law that was supposed to "save lives" has never been applied, the town keeps growing. The new mayor, Joseph Yannuzzi, recently told the press that "people come from the big cities to a small town for the schools and public activities. We have our problems, but Hazleton is safer [than those cities]."[7]

Even Congressman Barletta has acknowledged that the fact that the population of Hazleton grew for the first time in seventy years according to the 2010 census is a good thing. "It's good for us to grow, that helps to attract businesses to the city," Barletta stated in an article published in the *Hazleton Standard Speaker*.[8] The piece cites figures from the census, showing that the town had experienced net population growth for the first time since 1940. That growth is mainly attributable to the fact that by 2010, a full 40 percent of the city's residents were Latino.

Sosar believes the Latino population is really closer to 50 percent. Other cities in the surrounding area have also experienced similar population growth and revitalization, with more children attending local schools. Higher numbers of residents means more federal dollars for schools, Medicaid, and foster care, among other programs.

From time to time, blind panic over the "illegals" in Hazleton still strikes at Barletta, who during a speech on the floor of Congress told a story about a man in his district who had been pulled over for speeding, didn't speak any English, had a record, was unemployed, didn't know where he lived, and carried two cards for public assistance benefits. Still, the Immigration and Customs Enforcement didn't arrest him. "We shouldn't let people like that defraud millions of American taxpayers," Barletta admonished.[9]

Barletta keeps citing anecdotes instead of facts and figures, making the broad and erroneous assumption that undocumented immigrants do not pay any taxes, and picking isolated, aberrant cases to represent an entire community. And that's how he propelled himself to a seat in Congress in the United States House of Representatives.

NINE
ARIZONA, ALABAMA, AND KOBACH'S ANTI-IMMIGRANT LAWS

ARIZONA MAY BE KNOWN TO SOME AS THE HOME OF THE GRAND CANYON OR THE birthplace of labor activist Cesar Chavez. The very word "Arizona" conjures up sepia-toned images of the Old West and the shoot-out at the O.K. Corral, an epic gun battle brought to the silver screen by director John Ford starring such classic, red-blooded leading men as Henry Fonda, Burt Lancaster, and Kirk Douglas.

But in recent years, this legendary southwestern state has earned a very different reputation: as the battleground for a legal and political war that may change not only the law but also the very spirit of the United States as a land of immigrants. The Arizona State Legislature has been hard at work churning out a seemingly endless series of laws aiming to control immigration and punish undocumented immigrants. The measure that has gained the most attention—so far—is SB 1070, known as the Arizona Law.

The most controversial clause in the law, which was passed in 2010, not only permits but *requires* local police officers to confirm the immigration status of anyone during a routine stop. Although an amendment was added after the initial legislation passed prohibiting the use of race or ethnicity as the sole justification for stopping someone, the law does not completely exclude using racial and ethnic profiling in its application. For that reason, critics continue to argue that the law promotes discrimination based on race or ethnicity and is therefore unconstitutional.

Although SB 1070 is the best-known and most widely discussed of Arizona's anti-immigrant laws, it is certainly not the first, nor will it be the last to wend its way through the legislative chambers in Phoenix. Some predecessors include a law passed in 2007 that sanctions employers of undocumented immigrants, and Proposition 200, a referendum approved by voters in 2004 that would restrict undocumented immigrants' access to public services. Proposition 200 also required that anyone registering to vote must present proof of citizenship, such as a birth certificate or a passport.

Even though voting illegally has never been shown to be a strong motivating factor, compelling immigrants to risk their lives by crossing the border through Arizona's harsh desert and steep mountains, some politicians harp on the supposed threat to the integrity of elections to stoke Americans' fear of immigrants. In a country where the majority of eligible voters don't vote in most elections, it's ironic to think this argument might actually persuade anyone.

Proposition 200 was passed by 56 percent of voters amid assurances that it would protect the state budget from the hundreds of thousands of "illegals" who supposedly settle in Arizona just to get on welfare. But its effect on the immigration problem has been minimal at best. Most of the benefits it affects were already impossible for undocumented immigrants to obtain anyway, and the state attorney general, Terry Goddard, tried to mitigate its impact, asserting in a legal opinion issued after the vote, that no matter how independent Arizona might want to be, as a state it could not independently restrict access to federal services.

But according to journalist Valeria Fernández, who lives in Phoenix and writes on state issues, the real result of the measure was to "scare immigrants away from government offices, hospitals, and schools."[1]

Another important effect is voter intimidation. The use of laws to restrict access of certain minority groups to the vote is a well-known, time-honored tradition in US history, one that has been roundly condemned by the courts time and again.

In October 2010, in a two-to-one decision, the Ninth Circuit Court of Appeals struck down Proposition 200. The judges concluded, not surprisingly, that it violated the National Voter Registration Act of 1993, which sought to make voter registration *more* accessible, not less. The Ninth Circuit's ruling did not deter Arizona. The attorney general's office promptly announced plans to petition for a new hearing, before a larger panel of judges.

Arizona passed one controversial measure after another, including one that denies the right to bail for all undocumented prisoners and another that prohibits undocumented workers from suing or seeking damages, even if they are injured while on the job. But in March 2011, with its most controversial law still tied up in the courts and the state facing a serious budget crisis, the state legislature, with support of Democrats and a handful of Republicans, voted several anti-immigrant measures down.

It is not clear whether the legislative initiatives that have passed have resulted in substantially shrinking the population of undocumented immigrants in Arizona. In any case, just as with California's Proposition 187, at the very least, Arizona's measures serve as a precedent for similar laws and help sanction a radically anti-immigrant environment. These laws do not seem to be particularly effective, however, in solving the fundamental problems that encourage illegal immigration due to the absence of a coherent national policy.

On April 23, 2010, Governor Jan Brewer, a Republican in the middle of a reelection campaign and with few tangible accomplishments to her credit, signed the Arizona Law into effect with great fanfare. The auspicious event was splashed across the local news and covered in the national and international media. SB 1070 was sponsored by Republican State Senator Russell Pearce, a controversial figure with a colorful personal history as a veteran, former police sheriff, and leader in the struggle against the "illegal invasion," in his words.

SB 1070 goes much further than any other law in authorizing any local police officers to act as immigration agents as they go about their jobs. According to the federal Congressional Research Service, SB 1070 is an open challenge to the numerous legal precedents established over the years that limit the power of states and local municipalities to enforce federal immigration law. Enforcing those laws is a matter that should be left to the federal government, not local authorities, according to judicial decisions reached in courtrooms across the country.[2]

The Arizona Law has not only inspired copycat initiatives in a dozen states across the country, it also served as a political platform for Pearce, boosting his profile as he geared up for a run for a congressional seat in 2012. After SB 1070 passed, Pearce, elected state senate president, introduced increasingly radical anti-immigrant legislation, including an initiative to deny birth certificates to children of undocumented immigrants in the state of Arizona meant to force lawsuits and an eventual reconsideration of the Constitution's Fourteenth Amendment if the issue reached higher court.

No one else can take as much credit for Arizona's hard-line measures against undocumented immigrants as Pearce. On the biography page of his personal website, written in the first person, he describes himself as "one of the most outspoken advocates for stopping the illegal invasion, securing our borders and enforcing our laws."

But his obsession goes deeper than a simple desire to enforce the law or mere political opportunism. Pearce has made the issue the central theme of his career, and he has been behind almost all of the punitive measures introduced against undocumented immigrants in the state, from Proposition 200 to SB 1070, and three measures passed by voters in 2006, including an amendment to make English the "official language" of Arizona as well as the other two previously mentioned in this chapter.

Pearce seems to view undocumented immigrants as the root of all evils in Arizona, and hunting them down and banishing them seems to be his life's purpose. Perhaps that's why in the second paragraph of his biography, right after talking about his storied family tree ("My Great Uncle Joe Pearce was one of the original Arizona Rangers serving from 1901 to 1909 when they were disbanded; he was the last of the original Rangers to die," he writes), Pearce describes in detail an incident that occurred in 2004, when his son, a deputy for the Maricopa County Sheriff's Office, was shot by an "illegal alien." "I was in Washington D.C. at the time testifying about our nations [sic] failed immigration policies when I was handed a note and told there was an emergency at home and to call immediately. I called home and was told Sean was critically wounded after being shot in the chest and stomach and was being transported to Maricopa County Medical Center."

Pearce himself had worked in law enforcement for twenty-three years, reaching the rank of chief deputy in the Maricopa County Sheriff's Office, where the current sheriff is another notorious anti-immigrant hard-liner, Joe Arpaio. Pearce had also been wounded in the line of duty, although the only incident he mentions specifically is his son's shooting, which clearly changed his outlook on life and pushed him into a state of permanent outrage. It's as if from that day forward, all undocumented immigrants represented the man who fired on and almost killed Russell Pearce's son.

The day after the signing ceremony for SB 1070, the Los
Angeles daily *La Opinión,* the largest Spanish-language newspaper in the United States, ran the headline "Arizona, Hostile Land"
over its six-column front-page coverage. On May 1, protests were
staged in opposition to the law in cities across the country. But
polls showed that the majority of Americans actually supported
legislation like the Arizona Law, even as the same polls, para-
doxically, also showed that most responders favored measures
that would provide a path to citizenship to undocumented immigrants.[3] In Arizona, it was clear that only one side of the argument was represented in the halls of political power: nativism and
restriction.

Officially named the Support Our Law Enforcement and Safe
Neighborhoods Act, SB 1070 is the most restrictive and sweeping
anti-immigrant legislation to have passed in the United States recently. It unleashed a fierce controversy, and its legal consequences
are still reverberating in judicial chambers across the country. As
its name implies, the act was conceived as the way to reestab-
lish law and order in the state, key in the fight against a growing population of undocumented immigrants, who politicians like
Pearce and Brewer blame for almost all the economic and social
ills of society that they cannot—and do not even attempt to—
solve themselves.

The origins and intentions of SB 1070 are somewhat Ma-
chiavellian and cannot be strictly attributed to Pearce. The legislation itself was actually written by Kris Kobach, a lawyer, law
professor, advisor to Attorney General John Ashcroft during the
George W. Bush administration, and current Kansas secretary
of state. Kobach is the mastermind behind the Arizona Law
and other hard-line anti-immigrant legislation. His philosophy
is simple: "attrition through enforcement." He does not believe that one or two laws are going to solve the illegal immigration problem. Rather, the idea is to make day-to-day life so

unbearable for undocumented immigrants that they will decide to "self-deport" and leave the country, or in the case of SB 1070 the state, on their own.

According to the Center for Immigration Studies (CIS), the investigative arm of the Federation for American Immigration Reform (FAIR), pressuring undocumented immigrants to flee increasing persecution will be a cost-saving measure. FAIR purports to be a lobby group seeking to restrict legal and illegal immigration. In April 2006, CIS published a report explaining the virtues of this system of "self-deportation," arguing that enforcing the laws with an emphasis on deporting foreign criminal offenders "will only achieve limited results."[4]

"If supplemented by attrition through enforcement, which encourages voluntary compliance with immigration laws rather than relying on forced removal, the illegal population could be nearly halved in five years," the report states. It also asserts that applying this strategy throughout the country could result in the self-deportation of 1.5 million foreigners every year. With the passage of SB 1070, "attrition through enforcement" became official policy in the state of Arizona. The phrase is included in the law itself. That should come as no surprise; Kris Kobach, a former advisor to the Immigration Reform Law Institute (IRLI), the legal arm of FAIR, conceived and drafted SB 1070 and numerous other local measures enacted by municipalities trying to take control of immigration law (starting with Hazleton, Pennsylvania, in 2006).

FAIR presents itself as just one more Washington-based organization lobbying for enforcement of immigration law. But the Southern Poverty Law Center, a long standing civil rights organization whose main goal is to fight racist groups, characterizes FAIR as a group with definite white-supremacist leanings and the leader of the "neo-Nativist" movement that has been growing in recent years. In 2007, the center added FAIR to its list of hate groups. FAIR, IRLI, U.S. English (a group trying to make English the official language of the country), and several other related organizations were all founded by the same person: John Tanton, a retired ophthalmologist from Michigan. He started his political involvement in the 1960s as an activist for the Audubon Society and the Sierra Club, primarily concerned with the effects of overpopulation on the environment. Somehow this preoccupation morphed into genuine alarm regarding the "Latin onslaught," as he describes in a once-secret 1986 memo:[5]

"Gobernar es poplar [sic] translates 'to govern is to populate' . . . In this society where the majority rules, does this hold? Will the present majority peaceably hand over its political power to a group that is simply more fertile?" In other writings, he expounds on the necessity of maintaining a white, Anglo-Saxon majority: "I've come to the point of view that for European-American society and culture to persist requires a European-American majority, and a clear one at that," he wrote in 1993.[6] This likely is the broader objective driving anti-immigrant organizations to impose further restrictions on the immigration system and institute new laws at the state and local level to construct a self-perpetuating system of "attrition."

Obviously this strategy is fraught with constitutional, ethical, and even moral problems, as evidenced by the heated controversy surrounding SB 1070, the international attention it received, and the over half a dozen lawsuits filed against it. In the days and weeks following Governor Brewer's signing of the law, which was set to go into effect in July 2010, seven lawsuits were filed against it, including one by the federal Department of Justice. The lawsuits argued that the Arizona Law delivers a frontal assault on various constitutional rights. Most anti-immigrant legislation passed at the local level ultimately has been struck down in court for violating one fundamental principle: the federal government's supremacy in regulating immigration. Critics also assert that the Arizona Law violates the First Amendment guaranteeing freedom of expression and freedom of association, the Fourth Amendment protecting against search and seizure without probable cause, and the equal protection clause of the Fourteenth Amendment.

On July 28, 2010, one day before SB 1070 was supposed to go into effect, US District Court judge Susan Bolton issued a temporary injunction preventing major components of the law from being applied, pending further evaluation by the court.[7] Beyond the arguments rooted in constitutional law or legal technicalities that make perfect sense to the lawyers but mean little to the general public is what the Arizona Law actually means for the country. Omar Jadwat, lawyer for the Immigrants' Rights Project of the American Civil Liberties Union, cogently sums up the law's implications: "Arizona's law is quintessentially un-American: We are not a 'show me your papers' country, nor one that believes in subjecting people to harassment, investigation and arrest simply because others may perceive them as foreign."[8]

Jadwat is mostly right, but he is wrong about one thing: There *are* people in this country who believe that discrimination and the subversion of constitutional rights are perfectly justified when it comes to undocumented immigrants. People with that mindset can be found beyond Arizona's borders, in the capitals of at least a dozen other states where copycat laws seeking to emulate Arizona have been introduced, and more are springing up every month.

There are people who believe that there should be one powerful constitution protecting the rights of some but not all. Throughout the history of the United States, there has always been a subset of people—usually politicians—who believe it is possible to win elections by explicitly marginalizing a certain group or using them as a scapegoat for all of society's ills. It's certainly not the first time the scapegoated group has been immigrants. But the current sustained attack that was first launched in the mid-1990s has been in effect for over fifteen years now, and it could have decisive consequences for society as a whole and particularly for Latinos, the country's fastest-growing minority group.

SWEET HOME ALABAMA?

In the fall of 2011, Detlev Hager, an executive with Mercedes-Daimler Benz, was driving a rental car through the streets of Tuscaloosa, Alabama, when he was pulled over by a local police officer because of an irregularity with the license plates. Unfortunately for Hager, not only had he left his driver's license behind, he didn't have his German passport with him either. All he had was some German-issued identification in his wallet.

Hager had his run-in with the police just when this southern state with a dark past—the segregationist Jim Crow laws of a few decades earlier still reverberate in the memories of many—had begun implementing a new stringent anti-immigrant law. The measure was designed by the same lawyer who had written similar legislation for other states, including Arizona's SB 1070: Kris Kobach. The goal of the law, just as in Arizona, Georgia, and elsewhere, was to make daily life for undocumented so untenable that they would be forced to self-deport. To encourage this outcome, the measure included a series of clauses on policing the undocumented population, clauses that would have immediate consequences for Hager and others and would later have economic, social, and even diplomatic repercussions.

HB 56—known as the Alabama Law—passed after the Republicans won a supermajority in the Alabama state legislature in the 2010 elections and was signed by Governor Robert Bentley in June 2011. It was scheduled to go into effect on September 1 of that year but because of legal challenges was delayed until mid-October. Then, as a federal judge had done before, a court of appeals suspended part of the law while its constitutionality was evaluated, allowing other parts to go into effect. Even with only part of the law in full force, the Alabama Law was the harshest legislation of its kind passed by any state in the union, even more severe than its famous predecessor in Arizona.

HB 56 requires that the police ascertain the legal status of any suspect when he or she first comes into contact with the authorities, if there is a "reasonable suspicion" that the person may be undocumented. The law makes driving without a license a very serious transgression; severely punishes any transaction between an undocumented immigrant and a public servant; requires school districts to identify undocumented students and turn them over to state authorities; and bans all undocumented residents from receiving any state or local benefits.

The law contains so many clauses, so broadly framed, that it would be almost impossible for enforcement efforts not to impact in unexpected ways the immigrant population and others not included in the target group, as happened with Hagar and Ichiro Yada, an executive with Honda Motor Company who was arrested in Alabama the next week for the same reason. Yada's arrest was even more absurd, since he was carrying all of his documentation with him but nonetheless was fined. (The fine was later thrown out of court.) It's possible that the auto executive just looked too foreign to the bullheaded police officer who, it would seem, did not have a clear understanding of the law's specifics: Driving while being from another country was actually not against the law, just driving without documentation.

The stories of these two executives from the auto industry, which constitutes an important part of Alabama's economy and creates tens of thousands of jobs for the people of the state, made headlines worldwide. But they are just a symbol of how far-reaching and problematic the legislation is, although its sponsors assured the state legislature that it would create jobs. As soon as the Alabama Law took effect, reports of its real consequences quickly emerged: Immigrants left the state in search of somewhere less hostile to live; students were too afraid to go to school; water service was cut off to families in their homes; and indiscriminate use of racial profiling by the local police. The Justice Department's Office of Civil Rights received over one thousand complaints within just a few days of HB 56 going into effect.

Meanwhile, the godfather of the law, Kris Kobach, declared, "I'm proud to have been a part of it. And the untold story is how successful it has already been in opening jobs for Alabama citizens."[9] It was just this idea of a pro-job law that sold the state's legislators on it. At a time of soaring unemployment, undocumented residents were taking jobs that should have gone to Americans, the reasoning went. And just as has happened in other states, this theory has not been easy to verify. In fact, evidence suggests that the laws are having just the opposite effect: Farms and towns have lost a significant part of their specialized workforce; small towns that had been in decline and later revived by an influx of residents were once again struggling with an ebbing population; schools lost students; and terror has stricken the heart of the immigrant community and anyone who just looks like they could be a foreigner.

Just ask Carmen Velez, a Puerto Rican woman who went to renew her car tag at her local DMV (Department of Motor Vehicles) in Alabama. She was asked to present her birth certificate, and in spite of her protests, she went home and got it. When she returned to the DMV and presented the document to two different officials, she was told that it wasn't a US birth certificate.

"I thought they were joking with me. I couldn't believe it. I never thought they wouldn't know that Puerto Rico was part of the U.S.," Velez said in an interview with Maribel Hastings for her blog *America's Voice*.[10]

Governor Bentley did not take any action over the problems faced by Carmen Velez or the hundreds or thousands of other US citizens adversely affected by the law. But tensions with the auto industry and the possibility that the situation could affect Alabama's relations with other companies already operating in the state or considering doing so did touch the hearts—or the wallets—of high-level state functionaries. Where arguments against the law based on the devastating toll it was taking on immigrant families had no impact, another effect, the opposite of the job-creation engine Kobach had predicted, did make an impression: What if the law actually hurt Alabama's economy and, what's more, revived the racist image the state had tried to erase?

Aware of the state's segregationist laws of the not-so-distant past, and Alabama's role as the birthplace of the civil rights movement of the 1950s, Latino activists began to refer to HB 56 as the Juan Crow law. But Alabama's leaders insist that it's strictly a matter of jobs and enforcing the law. Nevertheless, unlike Arizona, which has a sizable immigrant population, and where many cities are grappling with large influxes of immigrants, in Alabama, the Latino population is a meager 4 percent of the total, concentrated in several cities and towns. Even with this small percentage, legal and undocumented immigrants were a vital part of Alabama's economy, and the agricultural sector in particular, which was the first area to be severely affected by the Latino exodus from the state.

Serious economists do not believe that the Alabama Law will create jobs; rather, they feel that it will result in a net *loss* of jobs. Laws that make the area a virtual police state, where even foreign business executives have to prove that they have permission to be in the country and are not just "one more illegal stealing an American's job," do not make an area business friendly.

In fact, Alabama's troubled past and how it is reflected in current attitudes and laws could be an impediment to attracting foreign and domestic investment. In the early 1990s, when Mercedes-Benz was considering opening a plant there, a high-level executive at the German firm repeatedly expressed his concern over the state's recent past, activities of local racist groups like the Ku Klux Klan, and the fact that the Confederate flag, a symbol of slavery, still hung at the state's capitol. According to press reports from 1993, then-governor Jim Folsom ordered the Confederate flag to be taken down, expressly to soothe any anxieties the motor company had over doing business in the state.[11] Modern Germany is, of course, particularly sensitive to its image in terms of racism and restrictionist laws against certain ethnic minorities because of its own Nazi past.

But in the South, a segment of the population still reveres the Confederate flag, viewing it as having historic significance, a symbol of southern pride and of a state's right to govern itself however it chooses. From a cultural standpoint, however, the Confederate flag is something more: a symbol of racism, exclusion, and nostalgia for a past when those concepts were seen in a more favorable light.

If it is in fact true that the new immigration law does not have anything in common with the Confederate flag and the state's segregationist past, nevertheless, the negative economic effect could be much more pronounced than any supposed positive effect of "opening up jobs for citizens," an elusive outcome that has not been verified in any of the states where this kind of law has been enacted.

Keivan Deravi, an economics professor at Auburn University in Montgomery, Alabama, and advisor to the state legislature, told a local newspaper that the idea that once immigrants leave, things would get better for everyone else "is not based on any type of research or economic theories."[12]

When immigrants depart, they leave behind not only vacant jobs but work left undone and labor insecurity for business owners. They take their families and their children, who leave school, which often results in a reduction in state funds allocated to local school systems. When immigrants leave, consumers and taxpayers are leaving as well, economists agree.

Beyond the law's impact on taxes and worker productivity there is a perception among would-be investors and companies that Alabama is turning back the clock. "How does this affect Alabama's image, a state with a controversial past that is once again willing to use the law to discriminate against a politically marginalized group?" asks Chris Westley, an economist at Jacksonville (Florida) State University.[13]

Business groups in Alabama asked for changes to the law, stating that it was already having a negative impact on job creation. According to an article published in the *Montgomery Advertiser,* foreign investors had expressed their discomfort about the law's implications for any investments they already had in Alabama.[14]

For example, the mayor of Thomasville, a town near Montgomery, said that the Alabama Law and the specter of the state's past was coming up in conversations with foreign companies that were looking to open overseas operations.

"Up until a few months ago no one mentioned it, but now it has come up several times, about the anti-immigrant law," Mayor Sheldon Day said. "It's reviving the old stereotypes that took us so long to overcome."[15]

Just a few weeks after the law went into effect, putting Alabama front and center on the world stage for marginalizing a minority group by criminalizing immigrants, Governor Bentley was forced to call foreign business leaders and reassure them that "we are not anti-foreign companies, we are very pro-foreign companies."[16]

The state attorney general even began to urge that changes be made to the law to eliminate certain sections, in particular the clause requiring public schools to collect information on which students were undocumented—a section that the federal courts suspended almost from the beginning.

Meanwhile, other states are taking full advantage of the chaos in Alabama. A few days after the German executive was arrested, the *St. Louis Post Dispatch* in Missouri ran an op-ed piece titled "Hey, Mercedes, Time to Move to a More Welcoming State": "We are the 'Show Me' state, not the 'show me your papers' state," the article said.[17] Its invitation to the company to locate its new plant in Missouri demonstrated that the Alabama Law, at the very least, is not the best public relations campaign on which to build a region's economic future.

TEN
THE BOOMING BUSINESS OF IMMIGRANT DETENTION

IN MID-MARCH 2012, ON A HOT DAY IN ARIZONA, MORE THAN EIGHTEEN HUN-
dred local, city, state and federal law enforcement employees and
industry leaders flocked to Phoenix for the Border Security Expo,
where the very latest technology in this growing field was on
display.

Drone aircraft, heat-sensitive goggles, infrared night-vision
cameras, and radars vied for attention, sophisticated machinery
developed by companies that see border security as a profitable
business of the present and the future. As military spending for
the wars in Iraq and Afghanistan dwindles, these companies are
hastening to explore new markets and opportunities.

The industry sees abundant opportunity in border protection,
because government spending is not declining in this area, but
just the opposite: Over the past decade spending has steadily increased, and that trend will only continue. In early April 2012,
the Border Security Expo's Twitter account proudly announced
that its 2013 convention was already 40 percent sold to vendors,
within just days after the current year's expo closed. In another
message to its fans, the expo optimistically outlined the future
for this bright industry: "The U.S. spends 5.5 billion dollars on

National Security, and that is projected to increase to 10 billion dollars over the next few years."

In fiscal year 2012 alone, the US government spent $4 billion on technology for national security. Part of that money, $1.5 billion, was allocated for constructing a new "virtual wall" along the Mexican border. The first time the project was attempted, the government spent over $1 billion on a contract with the giant Boeing Corporation. After five years of delays, budget overruns, and changes to the terms, the government had to cancel the contract, after only fifty-three miles of the Arizona border with Mexico had been fenced.

Corporations are lining up to compete for the money: General Dynamics Corporation and EADS, a European defense contractor, are bidding jointly; Lockheed Martin, Northrop Grumman, Raytheon, and once again Boeing will all bid for the massive contract.

Regulating and applying restrictions to immigration and detaining, imprisoning, and deporting immigrants is one area where commerce and government intersect and where action on a policy arena can bring great profit to an industry.

Astute corporate executives forecast a rosy picture: "I can only believe the opportunities at the federal level are going to continue apace as a result of what's happening (in Arizona with SB 1070). Those people coming across the border and getting caught are going to have to be detained and that for me, at least I think, there's going to be enhanced opportunities for what we do," explained Wayne Calabrese, president of GEO Group, a corporation that constructs, buys, and manages private prisons.[1]

Calabrese made those comments in May 2010, a short time after Arizona governor Jan Brewer signed SB 1070 into law.

The federal government's large and growing investment in border protection and detention and deportation of immigrants is one of the most important areas of job creation, generating lucrative contracts for private companies and the public sector. But private businesses—and labor unions representing immigration and border control workers—can be closely tied to the advancement of government policies designed to arrest, detain for lengthy periods, and deport increasing numbers of immigrants.

The fact that Arizona is at the epicenter of this thriving industry is no accident. Arizona was the first state to develop its own laws targeting undocumented immigrants. The Arizona Law was passed in 2010, about fifteen years after that state became the most popular route for illegal immigration, following the 1996 passage of the Illegal Immigrant Reform and Immigrant Responsibility Act and Operation Guardian, which effectively sealed off California's border and redirected the flow of crossers through Arizona's deadly mountain and desert terrain.

But the hardening of policies on the state level did not happen in 1996. It is happening now, in the midst of a stubborn economic recession, when the numbers of border crossers has dropped precipitously and when the prison population is shrinking as a result of lower crime rates and because states are cutting budgets and releasing nonviolent offenders to cut costs. In other words, the hardening of immigration enforcement comes at a time when for-profit border security interests and private prison management companies are actively seeking out new markets for their services and products. It is a market that, according to investigative reports, they helped to create.

Jan Brewer gave the keynote address at the 2012 Border Security Expo, almost two years after signing SB 1070, which was passed to intensify the persecution of undocumented immigrants and increasingly involve local police in their identification. The law could greatly increase the number of immigrants who are detained and deported.

Brewer is closely connected to the private prison industry. Her spokesman, Paul Senseman, as well as her campaign director, Chuck Coughlin, were both former lobbyists for private prison companies. Aside from these links, there are signs that the prison industry did more than just suggest that a law such as SB 1070 be enacted: It might have had a direct hand in pushing for and even drafting the legislation.

An investigation spanning several months conducted by National Public Radio (NPR) and published in October 2010 revealed the process through which Russell Pearce, former senator from Arizona and a principal architect of SB 1070, presented the idea for the measure to a group meeting in a conference room at the Grand Hyatt Hotel in Washington, DC, in December 2009. Some among the group were affiliated with the American Legislative Exchange Council (ALEC).[2]

ALEC brings together state legislators, representatives of interested corporations, and other associations. In that room where Pearce waited to lay out his vision for the state law, crafted with the help of Kansas State Attorney General Kris Kobach, also were representatives from the private prison industry, in particular CCA, the Corrections Corporation of America, the biggest company of its kind in the country.

Not only did they discuss what the proposed law would cover, they also went over the exact language of the draft legislation, which would serve as "a model" for the Arizona Law and others that they wanted to see pass all across the country. After discussing the details, there was a vote that unanimously supported the model. "No one voted no," Pearce told an NPR reporter. "I never had one person speak up in objection to this model legislation."[3]

In the same report, ALEC spokespersons acknowledged that part of their work is to bring business interests and legislators together in the same room, sitting around the same table, to talk about proposed legislation and even to reach a consensus in drafting and editing the exact text of the laws. This process is perfectly legal under United States law.

The potential influence of ALEC went beyond that meeting in Washington DC, thousands of miles from Arizona's border. Most of the thirty-six cosponsors of the bill in the Arizona state legislature had attended that ALEC meeting, and of those, thirty received donations from lobbyists connected to CCA and the GEO Group, another big private prison company within a few months. SB 1070 landed on Governor Brewer's desk in April 2010, and she promptly signed it into law.

According to a report issued by Public Campaign, an organization advocating reform of campaign contribution laws, lobbying by prison corporations is strategic, since they have political action committees (PACs) and also contribute directly to candidates who support their interests.[4] For example, PACs and executives of the private prison industry across the country have donated at least $3.3 million to parties, campaigns, and other PACs since 2001. The prison industry has also donated $7.3 million to candidates and parties on the state level since 2001. These local donations rose notably by $1.9 million in 2010, the same year the Arizona Law passed.

"It is hard to know just how much these companies really spend since their finances are not transparent, precisely because they are private companies and not public entities," points out Emily Tucker at the Detention Watch Network.[5]

What is very clear is that companies like Geo Group and CCA, the two biggest players in the private prison business in the United States, have enjoyed great success in recent years. It's a very healthy business climate for them, and they do not seem to have felt any ill effects from the recession. In fact, GEO Group and CCA have experienced a recent growth spurt. This growth did not stem from state-level contracts, since many states face serious budget shortfalls, but from contracts with the federal government, especially for immigrant detention centers.

Until recently, three main companies in the country were dedicated to constructing, renovating, and administrating private prisons and won public government contracts: CCA, GEO Group, and Cornell. Cornell was acquired by GEO in 2010, making CCA and GEO the two industry leaders.

The two companies had combined earnings of almost $3 billion in 2010 and controlled 75 percent of the private prison market. Most of their contracts are for state prisons, but, as mentioned, that is not where their future lies, since state governments currently do not have funds for new prisons.

Since 2001, CCA's earnings have increased by 88 percent, while GEO's earnings grew by 121 percent. GEO is a multinational corporation that also manages immigrant detention in other countries. For example, GEO manages a prison for immigrants in Scotland located in a castle that used to belong to a duke, who used it for hunting expeditions in the countryside. Now it belongs to the government of Great Britain.

In the United States, the detention of immigrants has increased steadily since 1996: The number of immigrants detained for immigration infractions has tripled since that date. Over the past five years the number doubled, according to an analysis conducted by the Detention Watch Network.[6] Every year US authorities detain at least 300,000 immigrants in contracted state prisons, private detention centers, and various centers that the federal government directly oversees.[7]

Cuts in state spending for prisons and the budget crisis that state and local governments are grappling with have translated into new opportunities for companies in the flourishing immigrant detention field. And the federal government's investment in more prison beds, contracting space that is left vacant in public prisons by the budget cuts implemented by states and local governments, and the construction of new immigrant detention centers all point to a very bright future for private corporate interests.

In a recent issue of its internal magazine, *GEO World,* GEO Group revealed that it would reap substantial rewards from two new facilities that it would be managing for the federal government: one in California and the other in Texas.[8] The article describes how the company was finalizing the renovation of the Adelanto Processing Center in southern California for a federal client, with a 650-bed capacity.

This project represented a significant amount of money for the company: Between contracts for the two facilities, GEO's earnings would increase by $15 million annually. To ensure that former prison employees did not lose their jobs, Adelanto won a contract with Immigration and Customs Enforcement (ICE) to install an immigrant detention center there, and GEO was subcontracted to manage it, adding an additional 650 beds to the existing capacity of federal immigration detention.

GEO is striking similar deals with states and counties around the country for new federal immigrant detention centers. According to GEO, the center in Texas will be "a new civil detention center" for "low-risk" immigrants—that is, not criminals.

CCA is actively seeking to turn local budget crises to its own advantage, expanding its business and winning the right to manage more prisons that currently are under public jurisdiction. In 2011, CCA sent letters to forty-eight state governments, offering to help them fill state coffers by buying the prisons the governments could no longer afford to manage. In exchange, CCA requested binding contracts to administer the prisons for at least twenty years and a guarantee that the states would keep the prisons at a minimum of 90 percent occupied for the duration of the contract, which is crucial because CCA is paid on a per-prisoner basis.

CCA asserts that turning the prisons over to them would save states a substantial amount of money over the long term, and several states have already taken the bait. But various state reports have shown that selling prisons to private corporations does not necessarily result in a savings for taxpayers.[9] It is more costly than for states to run them, because even when the private company manages the prison and the inmate population, the state still has to pay for medical care, which the private companies do not include in their services but which the state is obligated to provide. And once a corporation buys a prison, the state loses control over its inmates, since it is not so simple to cancel a contract when the facility becomes the corporation's private property.

Another indication of the cozy relationship between the government and corporations is the fact that many former government officials go on to become lobbyists for the very companies whose work they oversaw while in government. In their new, lucrative positions they influence former coworkers on the payroll of private companies that benefit handsomely from that influence. This "revolving door" of government and lobbying activities happens in all areas of the economy, and national security and border control is no exception.

There is nothing new about private and public interests aligning to achieve public objectives; such alliances have existed since the nation's founding. But the influence and involvement of the private sector in the areas of criminal justice and border control has grown in recent decades. The players move easily back and forth between public and private spheres, a phenomenon ethics watchdogs call the revolving door.

"Right now we are analyzing the relationships these companies have with present and former government officials in immigration," explains Emily Tucker, an investigator with the Detention Watch Network.[10]

Almost all industries have their own revolving doors: former government officials who go to work for private companies and who function as lobbyists or advisors on how to influence the areas of government in which they themselves are expert.

One example is Julie Myers, who was the assistant secretary for Homeland Security for ICE under the George W. Bush administration. She is currently a lobbyist for GEO, after GEO bought another company called Behavioral Interventions (BI), for which Myers was previously a lobbyist. BI developed alternatives to incarceration, including electronic monitoring devices that are strapped to the ankles of some immigrant detainees who are released from custody on bail. The use of technologies that provide alternatives to detention of immigrants, like the ankle bracelets, is a growing part of the detainment business, as the Obama administration is under political pressure to come up with more humane ways to detain low-risk immigrants.

Another example is former secretary of Homeland Security Michael Chertoff. His private company, the Chertoff Group, offers consulting services to giant defense and security corporations while Chertoff, who sits on the boards of several security and defense companies, advocates in the media for policy measures to shore up national security. A third example is Harley Lappin, chief corrections officer at CCA, who was formerly the director of the Federal Bureau of Prisons.

Government officials often move to the private sector for a while, only to eventually return to a position in government once their political party returns to power and hands out nominations. The Center for Responsive Politics, which studies the relationship between politics and influence, and money, explains what happens:

Although the influence powerhouses that line Washington's K Street are just a few miles from the U.S. Capitol building, the most direct path between the two doesn't necessarily involve public transportation. Instead, it's through a door—a revolving door that shuffles former federal employees into jobs as lobbyists, consultants and strategists just as the door pulls former hired guns into government careers. While officials in the executive branch, Congress and senior congressional staffers spin in and out of the private and public sectors, so too does privilege, power, access and, of course, money.[11]

Militarizing the border and detaining and locking up immigrants for long periods will not solve the problem of illegal immigration in the short or the long term. But these methods do generate billions of dollars and political benefits for the people who are constantly passing through that revolving door and the corporations that pay them.

ELEVEN
REJECTING EXTREMISM AND THE SEARCH FOR SOLUTIONS

The facts are incontrovertible that allowing an illegal invasion of the United States will destroy the American Southwest, and very probably wipe out the freedoms we American Christians enjoy, as Muslim Extremists blend in with the so-called "innocent" illegal aliens, and eventually proselytize them.

—Tim Donnelly, California assemblyman, founder
of the Minuteman Party, October 2010

You can't round up 12 million people to ship them across the border. That's a disaster. We need comprehensive immigration reform with a path to citizenship.

—Jerry Brown, Governor of California, February 2012

TIM DONNELLY TRIUMPHED IN THE CALIFORNIA ASSEMBLY ELECTION OF November 2010, winning a seat in a conservative district in the San Bernardino Hills, an hour away from Los Angeles. His identification with the Tea Party movement, then at the height of its popularity since it first splashed onto the national scene in 2009, certainly helped propel him into office.

The Tea Party had been born as a movement parallel to but separate from the Republican Party, although it espoused many traditionally conservative Republican views, such as fiscal conservatism and low taxes. Of populist origins, the Tea Party, which is not an actual political party, tends to reject the Washington "elite," instead supporting candidates of a more libertarian ideology. Texas congressman Ron Paul, a candidate for the Republican nomination in 2008 and 2012, is the best-known example.

Although it began as a movement focusing on fiscal issues, arguing against excessive spending and in favor of greater individual liberties, part of the Tea Party has become increasingly preoccupied with racial issues. From that perspective, Tea Partiers scrutinized and cast into doubt the authenticity of President Barack Obama's birth certificate, launching a protracted legal and media skirmish over the veracity of the document and the legality of his presidency (the Constitution requires the President to be born in the United States). At the same time, many leaders and followers of the Minuteman movement, the self-styled militias patrolling the border that had been running out of steam, took refuge in new Tea Party groups. Some, like Tim Donnelly, found a ready-made platform from which to launch political careers that were immediately successful, thanks to the sustained media attention and political relevance of the Tea Party.

On his website, Donnelly appears superimposed over an image of the Constitution, with the simple slogans: "Send a Minuteman to Sacramento" and "Patriot, not Politician." And with that his Minuteman past became entwined with the Tea Party, an informal alliance that was not looked on happily by everyone within the party. Nevertheless, the Minuteman activists, with their aggressive anti-illegal immigration message, infused the growing Tea Party's demonstrations with enthusiasm and attracted even more media attention, contributing to its notoriety and political successes.

Donnelly, who lives in the small mountain community of Twin Peaks near Lake Arrowhead in the San Bernardino Mountains, did not possess reserves of wealth or political experience. But his populist message and his plan to introduce a version of Arizona's immigration law SB 1070 in California struck a chord among many conservatives of his district, who already were concerned with the issue. It's worth noting that District 58, which Donnelly represents, is solidly Republican and its representatives are virtually always Republican.

A small business owner, Donnelly had been a Minuteman activist and the leader of the Minuteman Civil Defense Corps of California. In 2005, the group spent a week in the desert near the Mexican border, along with dozens of other volunteers, to carry out the "patriotic" mission of constructing a fence of metal and razor wire along parts of the nearly two-thousand-mile border.

This undertaking was lampooned a few times in 2006 and 2007 on *The Colbert Report,* a political satire show on Comedy Central. With his trademark straight-faced irony, Stephen Colbert pointed out that in the year after the four-hundred-yard fence—a full 0.2 miles—had been erected, it had successfully prevented three used plastic bags floating in the breeze from entering the country illegally. It was a funny way of saying the fence hadn't accomplished much of anything.

In any case, Donnelly's involvement with the Minutemen did help him win a seat in California's state capital in Sacramento. From there, he tried to convince his fellow legislators to pass more restrictive measures to counter what he characterized as the "illegal invasion." Donnelly found that by the second decade of the twenty-first century, California was no longer the fertile ground it had been for passing anti-immigrant measures. He repeatedly attempted but failed in passing legislation similar to Arizona's SB 1070, showing that not every region of the United States possessed the political will or virulent public sentiment necessary to follow the example set in Arizona, Alabama, Oklahoma, and Georgia, all of them states that passed local immigration control legislation in or after 2010.

Various states and cities across the country have rejected measures that many would qualify as extremist and anti-immigrant, and which constitutional legal experts argue go against the clause establishing the supremacy of the federal government in overseeing immigration control. At the same time, anti-immigrant measures advance elsewhere and the debate surrounding them wends its way through the courts, their fates to eventually be decided by the highest in the nation, the Supreme Court.

In his first two years as a state assemblyman, Donnelly did not have much luck in his efforts to bring the show-me-your-papers law to California. Two immigration bills that he introduced in 2011 did not even make it past a committee vote. The two measures, known as AB 26 and AB 1018, would have incorporated some parts of the law passed in Arizona into California law. For example, AB 26 would have granted any citizen the right to sue local governments that had a policy of sanctuary for immigrants and would have required private businesses to use the federal E-Verify system, an online system that allows employers to check the work eligibility of all prospective employees with government databases. The second would have required government agencies to use E-Verify. Critics allege that the system is plagued by errors and that its use lends itself to grave mistakes, such as keeping authorized workers from employment. Up until now, its use by employers has been mostly voluntary, although several states have passed laws requiring its use by all employers or by government contractors.

In California the committee vote that killed the two bills was along straight party lines: seven votes against from the Democrats and three in favor from the Republicans. Donnelly assured his district that he would keep trying. "This is not the end of the fight to protect citizens from the many problems caused by illegal immigration in California; I look forward to continued work on this critical issue. This is only the beginning of the fight," Donnelly told a local newspaper.[1]

The California legislature, controlled by a Democratic majority since the mid-1990s and with a large number of Latino legislators firmly opposed to any measures against immigrants, has rejected similar initiatives introduced by conservatives for years. And with Jerry Brown's election as governor in 2010 in the wake of Arnold Schwarzenegger's departure, conciliatory immigration measures began making it past the governor's desk and receiving approval. For example, Schwarzenegger had, during his term in office, repeatedly vetoed a law that would have given undocumented students access to private scholarships. That law, called the California DREAM (Development, Relief, and Education for Alien Minors) Act, was introduced by Los Angeles assemblyman Gil Cedillo again in 2011, and this time it passed both houses again but won the new governor's support, who said "going to college is a dream that promises intellectual excitement and creative thinking."[2]

Brown recognizes that the money California spends now educating those young people will result in more productive citizens, in terms of higher income taxes paid and other social and economic contributions to society overall. It's a bet on the future of thousands of undocumented students who eventually will be documented, unless the federal government decides to deport them en masse, which seems extremely unlikely. "The law benefits us all by giving top students a chance to improve their lives and the lives of all of us," Brown declared as he signed the law. California now allows undocumented students to apply for private scholarships as well as public grants.[3]

The negative backlash was not long in coming. Donnelly immediately launched a campaign to collect signatures to introduce a counterinitiative on the ballot in 2012 that would repeal the California DREAM Act. "All we need is 504,000 valid signatures, but I think we're probably going to get a million," Donnelly said, explaining that his office had received so many phone calls that nothing could keep the campaign from succeeding.[4]

He was wrong. As the deadline set by the secretary of state approached, Donnelly had not gathered enough signatures. His plan to defeat the California DREAM Act had been a resounding failure.

Things had changed significantly in California, the cradle of all the anti-immigrant movements spawned over the last twenty years. The reason: the growth of the Latino and other immigrant populations and their rise in political influence, coupled with a different attitude of the general population toward immigrants. It had been relatively easy to pass anti-immigrant measures in the 1990s, when voters' views on immigrants were generally negative. Today California, with more undocumented immigrants than any other state in the union, appreciates and accepts its undocumented people, and this has happened despite the events of 9/11 that hardened anti-immigrant policies in the nation at large. Polls of California voters, such as one conducted by the *Los Angeles Times* in 2010, found that attitudes had changed significantly from what they had been fifteen years earlier. Even in the midst of a recession, 59 percent of respondents favored the legalization of undocumented immigrants and 48 percent viewed undocumented immigrants as benefiting the country, while 32 percent considered them a burden.[5]

But California is not the only state where political changes can be seen in an overall rejection of anti-immigrant measures and movement toward laws that favor the integration of foreigners. In 2010 and 2011, as Alabama, Georgia, and Arizona went off in

one direction, Rhode Island went in another, and Utah tried to design more comprehensive, practical solutions to problems related
to the presence of an undocumented population.

In Rhode Island, the change coincided with the election
of a new governor, Lincoln D. Chafee, in November 2010.
Formerly a Republican senator representing his state, he had
left the Republican Party and declared himself an independent
a few years earlier. In his campaign for the governor's office,
he received the support of local pro-immigrant groups and the
growing Latino community in Rhode Island, which, although
still small, had grown by 40 percent over the past decade. The
entire state only has a little over 1 million residents, and of that
only 13 percent of the population is Latino, according to the
2010 census. But the presence of undocumented immigrants—
numbering between 20,000 and 40,000 according to various
estimates—had provoked several measures on the part of the
previous governor, Donald Carcieri, who argued they were a
burden on state budgets.

Carcieri had ordered all state agencies and contractors to use
the E-Verify database. He also supported granting state police
the authority to go after undocumented immigrants, a nationwide trend that many chiefs of police and experts in criminology
thought was diametrically opposed to the mission of police on
the local level and damaged their trust with the community. In
statements to the press, Governor Chafee said that the measures
implemented by his predecessor didn't accomplish what they had
set out to do: "The big thing was that it wasn't working. The idea
was that it would help us with our economy. It didn't accomplish
that."[6] As soon as he got into office, Chafee suspended the obligatory use of E-Verify, revoked the state police's authority to go
after undocumented immigrants, and openly supported a movement to give undocumented students financial aid so they could
go to college.

The issue does not always break down along predictable party lines. In Utah, an overwhelmingly Republican state heavily influenced by the Mormon church (the Church of Latter Day Saints), religious, community, and business leaders decided to tackle the immigration issue, resulting in a statement of five guiding principles called the Utah Compact. This agreement was criticized on both sides of the political divide for trying to marry respect for the law and border control to practical free market solutions while maintaining a humanitarian perspective. In the rest of the country, most other states marched in one direction: toward humanitarian or practical solutions—as, for example, in California—or toward an unending relentless attack on undocumented immigrants and promoting "self-deportation," a concept dreamed up by Kris Kobach, who, as discussed in chapter 9, said that each state had to make daily life ultimately so unbearable for undocumented people that they would have no other recourse other than to pack their bags and leave, "self-deporting" back to their country of origin.

The five principles of the Utah Compact were signed in Salt Lake City on November 11, 2010, by a group of religious, political, police, and community leaders. The agreement "urges" the federal government to try to find a national legal solution to the immigration issue and states that local police should focus on criminal activity, not civil violations of immigration law. It also called for a humanitarian approach that would not separate families while also recognizing the positive contribution that immigrants make to the US economy, even if they are not here legally. Such a recognition has been completely absent from discussion on the issue in Arizona, Alabama, Georgia, and other ideological disciples of Kobach, for whom the presence of undocumented immigrants is a clear negative for the economy and society. They are happy to ignore all the studies that have demonstrated a much more complex reality of costs and benefits that, if managed well, have been and can continue to be a real advantage for the United States.

Utah did not stop with approving this declaration of principles. The state legislature also passed a package of unprecedented immigration bills that were criticized by both extremes of the political spectrum. Unlike the Arizona Law and similar measures, Utah did not simply try to establish a police state or attack the problem by the force of the law; instead, it tried to find a way to bring immigrant workers out of illegality, recognizing how much the local economy may depend on them. Utah is an extraordinary case, not because it represents a clear solution to the problem that can be neatly applied in the other forty-nine states—it's not even clear that it will work in Utah yet—but because the legislature and the governor tried to silence all the empty rhetoric and give the anti-immigrant zealots a dose of reality. The United States has the right to protect its borders, but there are other realities and responsibilities that states cannot ignore. As of this writing, Utah is the only state in the union that has passed a state-administered temporary worker program.[7] It has also established an agreement with a state in Mexico that will supply the temporary workers.

The fact that this transpired in a solidly conservative Republican state, greatly influenced by the Mormon church—which 2012 Republican presidential candidate Mitt Romney belongs to and which has been divided on the issue—indicates just how urgent it is for the federal government to take action. Partial solutions are not enough, according to Utah governor Gary Herbert, who, to his credit, spoke in balanced, neutral terms throughout the discussion on the issue. "This is a very difficult emotional and complex issue and it has taken us as a country decades to be where we are today and we agree it's not where we want to be," Herbert said at a press conference after signing the package of laws. "Most of the frustration is now developing into anger, because the federal government has been on the sidelines not participating in the game on immigration reform, they haven't secured borders and developed no common sense immigration policy. I just want to commend our legislators for not shrinking from their responsibility on this, for going forward and making tough decisions to deal with this difficult issue."[8] The state of Utah is now negotiating with the federal government to get a waiver that would give it the authority to enforce a series of laws that, as in other states, generally fall under the domain of the federal, not state, government. They may never be applied—they are set to go into effect in 2013—but, in any case, Utah has established an alternative to the ineffective, partial political solutions.

Many other states have acted on their own, devising a variety of measures to solve what some view as problems caused by overly stringent laws: Where the federal government has made it mandatory to check employees' documentation using a national database, complaints about the excessive burden this requirement places on small businesses has prompted the passage of local laws creating exceptions to the rule and in some cases even prohibiting the use of the cumbersome system. Where the federal government has failed to pass a law for young undocumented students (a DREAM Act), many states have done so themselves, by offering students in-state tuition at public universities or access to publicly funded education grants, as California recently did. Where real or virtual immigration raids on businesses have resulted in pushing immigrant workers farther down the ladder to a shadowy employment market where they are more easily exploited than before, local initiatives try to force employers to follow minimum wage laws.

Laws that tackle only one side of the immigration issue do not always bring about the desired or promised results—this has been readily apparent in Georgia and Alabama, where harvests rotted in the fields for a lack of agricultural workers, for example. But one thing is certain: As long as Congress and the president fail to initiate meaningful, comprehensive immigration reform that goes beyond partisan rhetoric, states will continue to pass legislation on their own, further segmenting laws that affect immigrants and resulting in nothing more than what we already have: an incoherent collage of policies that does not solve the problem for immigrants, local economies, or the country as a whole.

PART III
DREAMS HAVE NO VISAS

TWELVE
IMMIGRANT YOUTH AND
THE BROKEN DREAM

*It's not me me me, it's not, give me residency, give me education . . .
it's give me the opportunity to go back to my communities and
make change, the opportunity to work for this nation, the opportunity to show other students the qualities that I have. It's not give me
money, education, it's give me the opportunity, let me have change,
let me create change.*

> —Grecia Lima, student at the University of California San
> Diego, 2008, activist in support of the DREAM Act

*The DREAM Act is a nightmare. With immigration back in the
news, proponents of the DREAM Act are again peddling arguments for a massive amnesty for millions of illegal immigrants. The
DREAM Act represents a dual assault on law-abiding, taxpaying
American citizens and legal immigrants.*

> —Republican Congressman from Texas and Chairman
> of the House Judicial Committee Lamar Smith, 2010

THE AFTERNOON TRAFFIC IN WESTWOOD NEAR THE UNIVERSITY OF CALIFORNIA'S
Los Angeles (UCLA) campus was even more backed up than usual
on May 20, 2011. The Los Angeles Police issued a transit alert to
the media stating that vehicular traffic was virtually at a standstill:

"Wilshire Boulevard, near the 405 exit and Veteran Avenue, is severely congested, use an alternate route."

This wasn't your typical traffic jam. The intersection, one of the busiest in the country, had been deliberately blocked by nine young adults sitting on the pavement all across Wilshire Boulevard. Wearing jeans and red T-shirts that read "The Dream is Coming," with graduation caps on their heads, they were surrounded by about fifty students, professors, and activists, carrying signs with messages of solidarity.

The nine main protestors were all college students, some undocumented themselves and others children born in the United States of immigrant parents. They protested to draw attention to the DREAM (Development, Relief and Education for Alien Minors) Act, a legislative initiative that had come before the US Congress several times since it was first introduced in 2001 and had yet to win enough support to become law. (The bill's original sponsor when it made its debut in August 2001 was Utah's Republican senator Orrin Hatch, who over the next decade would become an advocate of hard-line immigration policies, strict enforcement, and deportation.) If it became law, the DREAM Act would grant legal residency to young adults who met certain requirements as college students or by serving in the military.

On that May afternoon in 2011, the nine students were detained and fined by the California Highway Patrol. It wasn't the first time, nor would it be the last, that young people who had everything to lose would willingly risk arrest in an act of civil disobedience or protest, deliberately shining a spotlight on their own shadowy circumstances. Since that time, thousands of students and professors sympathetic to their plight have joined in the protests.

In recent years, the "Dreamers," as they call themselves, have gradually coalesced into a passionate national movement made up of countless young immigrants who only want to achieve their full potential but face insurmountable obstacles. They have testified before Congress, protested in legislators' offices, brought traffic to a halt, held protests and rallies at campuses around the country, and collected signatures in support of friends in deportation proceedings. Some have been deported themselves, while others have managed to avoid it, thanks to their network of supporters and their savvy use of social and traditional media.

Coming out of the shadows, openly declaring their status and telling their stories was the only way these students could build an effective movement. Many of the Dreamers decided to step forward, joining the vibrant activist movement that has become part of the national dialogue. They have courageously told their stories in newspapers, on television, and on the Internet. Groups of Dreamers have sprung up on college campuses in all of the fifty states. One by one, hundreds of students who had been quietly living in fear have decided to come out as undocumented, at a time when that label carries a huge stigma beyond mere social ostracism: To a certain vocal segment of the populace, "undocumented" is synonymous with "illegal" and therefore "criminal," no different from any other lawbreaker.

Before the Dreamers became known in the last few years, the media in the United States has generally focused on immigrant youth, particularly Latinos, strictly within the context of crime and gang violence, the Dreamers have started to shift that bias. In 2010, two student leaders came out of the immigrant closet at their campuses. Pedro Ramirez, twenty-two, president of the student council at Fresno State University, publicly confirmed his undocumented status in November after an anonymous email tip had been sent to the school newspaper and the *Fresno Bee*. Brought to the United States from Mexico when he was three years old by his parents, Ramirez, a political science major, says he had been unaware of his immigration status until he was in high school. He was able to pay for college with the help of private scholarships and working odd jobs. Once he openly admitted his status, he expressed an enormous sense of relief, after having lived with the secret for a few years. He had told university officials of his status when he ran for student council president, and they were supportive. But it was only after he won the election that he found out the job came with a stipend of about $800 per month, which he could not collect because he refused to lie about his status.

At a student rally at Miami Dade College in June 2011, Jose Salcedo, nineteen, made the same surprising announcement. Born in Colombia, Salcedo was president of the Student Government Association at the InterAmerican campus, student representative on the Miami Dade College board of trustees, and a member of the school's elite Honors College. Majoring in international law, Salcedo decided to take the risk and publicly disclose his undocumented status to illustrate very personally how critically important the legislation's passage is to hundreds of thousands of other students in the same situation. He told the stunned audience, "For ten years I've been scared to come out of the shadows. This is the first time I've spoken in public, telling people that I'm undocumented."[1]

Grecia Lima was one of the first Dreamer activists at the University of California at San Diego, and in 2008, at a conference organized by the university, she gave a moving speech.[2] Listening to her, one can sense the vast potential and energy being drained from this country's future if these young people cannot be completely integrated and accepted as full participants in our society. "Being an undocumented student, you live between privilege and marginalization. You come to a school filled with buildings that look like Hollywood and professors who are Nobel winners, you go back to your communities and you don't see change. I am so privileged to be a UCSD student, but I don't have enough resources to make all the changes."

In spite of Lima's excellent grades and intelligence, UCSD denied her an AMGEN scholarship. It wasn't anything personal: Undocumented students are ineligible for scholarships, just as most public and private financial assistance is out of their reach.[3] "I just want to say, let me share who I am. I want to do research, I want to do a doctorate in anthropology, but I can't. What am I going to do after graduation, where am I going to go? Why doesn't this country want me here? I don't understand."

Some may assume that these high-achieving undocumented students are isolated, exceptional cases. But the reality is that in an environment where challenges and obstacles outweigh opportunities by far, the emergence of numerous undocumented students with extraordinary academic and leadership achievements to their credit underscores the fact that the United States should make the most of this generation, a valuable human resource, to benefit its own national interests.

Another clear example is Walter Lara, one of the first undocumented students to be granted an indefinite stay of deportation in 2009, thanks to national fund-raising and publicity campaigns. His case opened the door for others. Walter had lived and studied in Miami ever since his family brought him there from Argentina when he was three. He always dreamed about going to school and working for the animation company Pixar. But once he understood that he was undocumented, without a social security number, he knew he wouldn't be eligible for any scholarships, and higher education would be extremely expensive.

He enrolled in college anyway and earned a degree in computer graphics with an impressive 3.7 grade point average. He had to get to work right away to pay off his bills, and he got a job installing satellite dishes while freelancing as a website designer. One day, on the way to an installation job, he was stopped and questioned by the police, and he admitted that he was undocumented. He was taken into custody.

He spent twenty days in an immigration detention center in Pompano Beach, where he met others just like himself who had been brought to this country when they were small and didn't know or remember anyplace else. The only country they knew was the one that wouldn't accept them. "It was really sad, there were kids in there who were younger than me, I remember one who was just sixteen, there were lots of Mexicans, Haitians, Argentinians, lots of Hispanics," Walter said in an interview with a local newspaper.[4]

Family and friends immediately sprang into action. US senator Bill Nelson (D-FL) was so moved by the case that he contacted the secretary of National Security, Janet Napolitano, and urged her to stop Walter's deportation proceeding, which was scheduled to take place on the Fourth of July weekend. Napolitano's office was also deluged with hundreds of phone calls from Walter's supporters.

On July 2, just a few hours before he was scheduled to be deported, Walter's order of deportation was suspended directly by Napolitano. A photo of Walter, taken by some activists who were with him when he got the news, shows him overcome with emotion, covering his face and sobbing with relief.

During its first three years, the Obama administration refused to issue an executive order to suspend the deportations of these young immigrant students. Even so, many Dreamers have been granted stays of deportation on a case-by-case basis. Lara was one of the first, and more have followed, although the government will not give out official information on the exact number of young immigrants who have been given a second chance. In August of 2011, the Obama Administration issued a "prosecutorial discretion" memo, outlining measures to prioritize the arrest or deportation of criminals and other high priority cases and setting up a system for review and identification of lesser priority cases and potentially administratively closing or suspending those of people without a criminal background and with deep ties to the country. The Dreamers became part of the group that were given a temporary reprieve, although their cases were still taken one by one and not permanently resolved. On June 15, 2012, President Barack Obama announced that his administration would stop deporting young undocumented immigrants who met certain conditions, granting them deferred action on a case-by-case basis. The estimates of how many "dreamers" would benefit vary between 800,000 and 1.4 million. But their status still is not permanent and could be overturned.

A more long-term solution would be in the best interest of the United States. Most comprehensive studies carried out on this issue indicate that making full use of these young immigrants' talents and abilities would have an unequivocally positive economic and financial impact on the country. Nevertheless, taking any definite action to help them would be a political risk that, it would seem, not even a Democratic president can afford to take. Polls show that a majority (54 percent) of Americans are in favor of the DREAM Act, but when broken down by political party or age, the results paint a different picture.[5] A clear majority of young and nonwhite (an official classification that includes a wide range of races and ethnic groups) people support it, but those are not the populations that generally have the strongest voter turnout.

As long as the sitting government fears the reactions of vocal minorities in key states, no matter which party is in power poll results will have no meaningful political impact. For the poll results to have any meaing, more moderates and independents have to be convinced of the DREAM Act's benefits for the country—something that has yet to occur. A clear majority of Americans has yet to understand that granting legal status to this powerful young generation wouldn't be anything more than an act of compassion. Critical analysis has shown that legalizing these young people is nothing short of an economic necessity for the United States.

WHAT IS THE DREAM ACT?

The last version of the DREAM Act legislation that was passed by the US House but rejected by the Senate (due to a Republican filibuster) in December 2010 would have provided undocumented immigrants who qualify a conditional, six-year path to citizenship, requiring completion of a college degree or two years of military service. To be eligible, immigrants:

- Must have entered the United States before the age of sixteen
- Must have been present in the country for at least five consecutive years prior to the enactment of the bill
- Must have graduated from a US high school or have obtained a General Educational Development (GED) diploma or been accepted into a college or university
- Must be between the ages of twelve and thirty-five at the time of application
- Must demonstrate good moral character

If the DREAM Act in this version ever passes, undocumented immigrants who qualify would have to enroll in a college or university to pursue a degree or enlist in one of the branches of the military. Within six years of approval for conditional permanent residency, they must have completed at least two years of study or military service. Once five-and-a-half of the six years have passed, they can apply for legal permanent residency and then citizenship. The exact number of undocumented immigrants currently enrolled in colleges and universities isn't known. Estimates of undocumented high school seniors graduating each year range from 25,000 to as high as 65,000,[6] and some estimates point out to as many as 2 million young people in this situation. Most of those students were brought to the United States as young children by their parents, who entered the country either illegally or with legitimate visas that later expired. The fact that they were undocumented did not have serious repercussions in childhood, because according to US law and particularly since the 1982 *Plyler v. Doe* decision, a state cannot deny a public education to any child, regardless of their immigration status.

The antecedents of the *Plyler* decision can be found in Texas in 1975, when the state approved a law denying a public education to undocumented children. Soon thereafter, the Tyler Independent School District decided to allow those students to enroll but charged them a $1,000 fee for the privilege. In 1977, a group of parents sued the superintendent of schools, James Plyler, and the local school board in federal court. A federal judge, the court of appeals, and finally, in a five-to-four decision, the US Supreme Court ruled that such laws were unconstitutional, violating the equal protection clause of the Fourteenth Amendment to the Constitution. Since that time, the *Plyler* decision has served as legal precedent guaranteeing the right to a public elementary and secondary education to all children residing in the United States, including those who are not in the country legally.

But the situation changes radically once these young undocumented immigrants reach adulthood or graduate from high school. For many, attending college or simply landing a job is an impossible dream. The *Plyler* ruling did not apply to higher education, especially after the Illegal Immigration and Immigrant Responsibility Act (IRAIRA) was passed in 1996, allowing states to restrict access to state colleges and universities based on immigration status. In certain states, undocumented high school graduates can attend state colleges, but they are not eligible for in-state tuition. Out-of-state tuition rates are prohibitively expensive for most children of immigrants, whose families generally occupy the lower rungs of the socioeconomic ladder. In California, for example, students who are state residents pay $11,300 for a year's tuition while out-of-state students pay $34,000 per year—three times as much.

On top of that, undocumented students are ineligible for public and many private scholarships. In California, a law was passed in 2011 that would change that situation, allowing undocumented students to apply for privately funded college scholarships. But in most states, undocumented students are not eligible for college scholarships.

During their childhood and teen years, most of these young people do not realize that they are at a serious disadvantage. Once they graduate high school and try to go on to college, they face a stark reality: They cannot obtain a social security number, a driver's license, or live a normal life. From then on, they have to exist in a kind of limbo.

"Being undocumented feels like being a kid forever: you can't get any government ID—any store, any bank, any transaction requires ID," explains Stephanie Solis, an undocumented student at the University of Southern California. When she was eighteen, her parents sat her down and told her that she did not have legal status in this country.

Solis has been lucky, relatively speaking. Since she lives in California, she can attend a state college paying the in-state tuition. California is one of eleven states that have passed laws specifically allowing undocumented students to pay the same as other resident students, along with Illinois, Kansas, Maryland, Nebraska, New Mexico, New York, Texas, Utah, Washington, and Wisconsin. In practice, undocumented students in Minnesota and Nevada can also pay in-state tuition.

In the rest of the states, undocumented students have to pay the same tuition as foreign students. Arizona, Colorado, Georgia, and Oklahoma have passed laws explicitly stating that undocumented students are ineligible for in-state tuition rates. In Alabama, the mere presence of undocumented students at institutions of higher learning is expressly forbidden. In South Carolina, they cannot attend any university no matter what they may be willing to pay—and the state of Georgia prohibits public universities from

enrolling undocumented students at any school where any qualified applicants have been rejected in the prior two years due to
lack of space.

The biggest challenge these students face may come after
graduating from college, if they manage to get that far: Their lack
of immigration status condemns them to life in an inescapable
underclass. Practically speaking, they cannot get a job to put the
skills and education they acquired in college to use.

Nevertheless, undocumented students keep forging ahead.
The press has reported many stories of remarkable achievements
of students without papers who graduated at the head of their
class, demonstrating extraordinary motivation. For example, in
2011, Isabel Castillo received an honorary doctorate degree from
the University of San Francisco in recognition of her academic
achievement for graduating with honors from the University
of Virginia and for her tireless work as an activist on behalf of
all undocumented students. In June 2011 José Antonio Vargas,
a Filipino American and Pulitzer Prize-winning reporter who
had worked for several important publications, including the
Washington Post, "came out" as undocumented in an essay written for the *New York Times Sunday Magazine.* He learned of his
status when he was 16 years old. He has since become an activist
and a face for Dreamers through his project "Define American."

Of course, not all undocumented students are high achievers.
But there are enough shining examples to suggest that decision
makers in this country should view this group of students as wor-
thy of recognition and do whatever they can to make sure their
talents and abilities are used to fully benefit the United States.

AN UPHILL ROAD

The DREAM Act has been pending in Congress for a decade. Its
most crushing defeat came hand in hand with its biggest triumph:
In early December 2010, the House of Representatives passed the

law for the first time, only to have it defeated in the Senate a few days later.

Even if it passes, the conditions that would have to be met under the DREAM Act in order to obtain temporary legal residency—two years of military service or two years enrolled in college—would not be easy to achieve, despite what the measure's critics allege would be an open door for general "amnesty."

After six years of temporary residency, immigrants would have to demonstrate passing grades in college or honorable service in the armed forces for a minimum of two years. For those in the military, their commitment would actually be much longer, because enlistment requires a contract of at least eight years; for soldiers on active duty, the minimum requirement is four to six years.

The DREAM Act has proven to be such a controversial topic that it has yet to reach the president's desk. It faces radical opposition: According to the most extreme groups that oppose it, such as Americans for Legal Immigration (ALIPAC), passage of the act would mean "the destruction of America."

"The America as you know it will be gone forever along with our borders," ALIPAC warns. In a message to its followers, the leaders of ALIPAC conclude: "Illegal aliens roam freely in America as unrestrained workers, students, and voters already. All Congress is really doing is giving a rubber-stamp legitimacy to the massive crimes already committed against America and Americans."[7]

The most radical groups put forth various theories on immigrants, depending on the audience. One such view asserts that undocumented immigrants come here to vote illegally and rig the US legal system in their own favor, although it would seem that until now, at least, that strategy has been completely ineffective at best, due to the lack of results or any clear cases of such fraud.

No reputable study carried out by any academic, nonprofit, or government institution in the country has demonstrated that undocumented immigrants actually vote. The real, undeniable problem is that most Americans who are eligible to participate in the country's democratic process and vote do not, and the "best democracy in the world" has abysmally low levels of voter participation in elections at all levels.

Although it seems laughable, the image of young immigrants as dangerous elements wandering the streets who—horror of horrors!—study, work, and vote in this country does have its audience. Even political moderates are openly concerned about immigrants draining money from public coffers, and in times of economic and budgetary crisis, they wonder if undocumented immigrants do not make things even worse.

The moderate critics of immigration—moderates at least in comparison to ALIPAC—use this fear as the basis for their arguments. Groups like the Center for Immigration Studies (CIS), the Federation for American Immigration Reform (FAIR), and Numbers USA promote the idea that the United States is suffering from massive, completely out-of-control immigration that will eventually destroy the country. All of the previously named organizations were founded by John Tanton, the ophthalmologist from Michigan who claims to be the "pro-immigrant founder of an immigration network," according to his own website.[8]

FAIR and CIS have taken a strong stand against the DREAM Act, saying that it would lead to the legalization of over 2 million illegal immigrants, giving them access to "in-state tuition rates at public universities, federal student loans, and federal work-study programs. Aliens granted amnesty by the DREAM Act will have the legal right to petition for entry of their family members once they become naturalized U.S. citizens," warns an analysis from FAIR, a restrictionist group.[9] Actually, the organizations' positions are designed more to generate an emotional response than to serve as well-reasoned, fact-based arguments explaining exactly how legalizing these students would hurt the country.[10]

Some in the Dreamer movement assume that the heart-wrenching, deeply personal stories of many of the Dreamers ultimately will prevail, generating enough sympathy to get the legislation finally passed. To many, it is nothing less than a civil rights movement that will have wide-reaching benefits for the country as a whole.

"A new civil rights movement is certainly under way," says Will Perez, a professor at the University of Claremont who has studied the Dreamers. "Forty years ago, landmark civil rights legislation not only improved the lives of 18 million African Americans—it also made the country better as a whole. Pragmatic immigration reform will not only benefit 16 million undocumented individuals and their US-born children but everyone in this country."[11]

Some of the Dreamers themselves think that the strategy to get the DREAM Act passed has focused too heavily on their individual stories and not enough on what the country as a whole actually stands to gain from passing the legislation.

"I think that to win the support of people who aren't really interested or aren't convinced, we need to address their concerns. So far the movement has said that the students need this law, I think it's better to say that the country needs *them*," says twenty-seven-year-old Edgar Santos from Los Angeles. Santos is producing a documentary about the Dreamer movement and has himself experienced living without legal status.[12]

"The opposition says the DREAM Act would be a nightmare for the United States, for budgets, for other students, for the economy. I believe you have to fight on their terms, you have to meet them where they live. You have to convince this older, suburban population, the ones who are on the fence. We have to sell ourselves like a product," Santos explains.

What is the product that the Dreamers are offering? Several studies carried out by reputable organizations not necessarily for or against the legislation shed light on what is at stake for the country.

For example, in 1999, the RAND Corporation concluded that in order to raise the graduation rates of Hispanics to those of white non-Hispanics, public education budgets would have to be increased by 10 percent. The positive effects that measure would have on the economy would easily justify the initial expense: "For example, a 30-year-old Mexican woman with a college degree would pay $5,300 more in taxes and would use $3,990 less in government services every year, when compared to someone without a high school degree," the RAND study pointed out.[13]

Better educational opportunities means better jobs, which means higher incomes and higher taxes paid. A UCLA study found that the group that stands to benefit from the DREAM Act would earn, in total, from $1.4 to $3.6 billion more than it would if the act wasn't passed. Another study conducted by the Community Colleges of California concluded that throughout their working lives, college graduates earn 60 percent more on average than high school graduates. And advanced degree holders can earn two or three times what high school graduates make.[14]

The simple act of legalization carries with it an increase in income: A Department of Labor study found that immigrants legalized by the amnesty law passed in 1986 earned 15 percent more over the next five years and immediately moved up on the labor scale.

Also, demographic analyses reveal a society that is aging, even when the presence of undocumented immigrants is taken into account. Dowell Myers, a demographer from the University of Southern California, argues that a new generation of workers is required to replace the aging of the baby boomer generation—those born between the end of World War II and 1964—who are now in their most productive years or entering retirement, something that will certainly not happen if these young immigrants are not included.

Today the ratio of seniors over the age of sixty-five to people in their most productive years is 240 to 1,000—what it has been since 1980; over the next twenty years, that proportion is expected to change to 411 elders to 1,000 active workers.

Meyers explains: "This aging demographic will need support, healthcare expenditures, and other benefits which will dominate the fiscal landscape of the country and that, according to the government's own studies, are 'unsustainable' under the current circumstances. And the exit of these people from the active workforce will be so massive that if they are not replaced at all levels, there will be serious consequences."

Meyers points out that young minorities and immigrants will play a very important role over the next few decades, and since those groups have higher birthrates than the rest of the population and belong to the fastest growing segment of the American population, they have the potential to become the new middle class of workers, taxpayers, and homeowners. To Meyers, failure to deliberately cultivate this new generation is not only wrong, it is dangerous.

Who will buy retirees' homes when they are ready to sell them? Who will foot the bill for social security for this massive group of senior citizens? Meyers explains, "The best thing we could do for the future of the United States is to think about how we can educate and maximize the participation of these new groups into our society and economy."

THIRTEEN
THE OBAMA ERA
A PERFECTED DEPORTATION MACHINE

FEW COULD HAVE ANTICIPATED THAT THE CHANGE BARACK OBAMA WAS SELLING during his successful 2008 presidential campaign with respect to immigration would not be comprehensive legislative reform but the perfection of a series of programs for arrest and deportation, programs initiated in prior administrations but now applied more efficiently and more quickly than ever before. More than 1.2 million undocumented people were deported during the first three years of the Obama administration. His critics have never acknowledged this milestone achievement, instead accusing him of offering "amnesty" and opening up the borders.

Latinos have been disproportionately affected by the deportations carried out under Secure Communities, the most widely used program by the Obama Administration to deport undocumented immigrants. Secure Communities is a system that allows state and local police to check the fingerprints of an individual they are booking into a jail against Department of Homeland Security (DHS) immigration databases. If there is a "hit" in an immigration database, Immigration and Customs Enforcement (ICE) is automatically notified, even if the person has not been convicted or even formally charged with a crime.

There have been many allegations of racial profiling in the application of this program, especially because most of the arrests are carried out by local and state police who often stop people for "looking" undocumented—as SB 1070 and other state immigration laws appear to encourage and book people in local jails for lacking a driver's license, the perception of a misdemeanor crime or even calling the police on a domestic violence incident. The large number of deportations of people with no criminal record generated the strong criticism of immigrant rights groups and many in the Latino community.

According to a report released in October 2011 by the University of California Berkeley law school and the Benjamin N. Cardozo School of Law in New York, 93 percent of immigrants arrested under Secure Communities were Latinos, although Latino immigrants only make up about two-thirds of all undocumented immigrants in the United States.

For months, while Immigration and Customs Enforcement (ICE) detained and summarily deported hundreds of thousands of immigrants—the majority of whom were workers whose only crime was having crossed the border illegally or overstayed a tourist visa—conservative media outlets warned about the "amnesty" the Obama administration was busily plotting. "Obama Using Bin Laden Momentum to Push for Amnesty for Illegals" screamed a provocative headline on the Fox News Channel in May 2011. "Obama Passes Amnesty by a Back Door ICE Directive" lamented the website for the conservative Tea Party movement, the *Tea Party Tribune*, on June 23, 2011.

During his first campaign for the presidency in 2008, Obama had promised to work on passing comprehensive immigration reform that would have legalized millions of undocumented immigrants and addressed the serious limitations that the complex patchwork of immigration laws pose for the social and economic life of the country. One of the many "changes" Obama offered voters was confronting the challenge of enacting urgently needed, balanced immigration law reform.

That clear commitment to actively pursuing immigration reform was a strong attraction for Latino voters, who had largely turned their backs on the senator from Illinois and thrown their support behind Hillary Clinton in the first Democratic primary.

The undocumented immigrant situation was at a critical point by the beginning of the twenty-first century. The Pew Hispanic Center, a research institute on social issues headquartered in Washington, DC, estimated that the population of undocumented immigrants had reached 12 million.[1] The system of immigration laws had been insufficient for effectively processing them for some time, and the booming economy of recent years—a bubble that would soon burst—had served as a beacon, drawing foreign workers to where the jobs were.

Thus, during the last few years, the immigration issue has played a much more critical role than it had previously in capturing the majority of the Latino vote: The more precarious the lives of undocumented immigrants became, and the more harassment they were subjected to, the more important a candidate's views on immigration were to Latino voters.

By the time Obama was anointed as the Democratic candidate in the summer of 2008, it was clear that the Latino vote was going to be an extremely important factor in the election, especially in states where it could just as well go to either party, such as Colorado, Florida, and New Mexico.

As the campaign turned into the home stretch, the country was in serious financial crisis, and the political mood reflected it. Because of rampant speculation and questionable lending practices, the real estate market had become overvalued, and the bubble finally burst in 2007, leading to the collapse of the banking industry in the fall of 2008, just as the presidential race reached its height.

The economic crisis arose almost in tandem with a rising back-lash against the growing presence of Latino immigrants in cities and towns in the nation's heartland. Punitive laws against their presence followed one after the other in those years. Spearheaded by Democratic senator Edward Kennedy and Republican senator John McCain, Congress debated whether to pursue comprehen-sive immigration reform or pass measures that would not only pe-nalize the undocumented immigrants themselves but anyone who aided them in any way.

A couple of years previously, the media seemed taken aback by a wave of pro-immigrant marches in Chicago, Houston, Los Angeles, and New York, attracting hundreds of thousands of participants. Immigrants and their supporters raised their voices and marched by the millions in the spring of 2006, but their de-mands and simply their visibility may have set off the backlash to come and the defeat in 2006 and 2007 of the last attempts at immigration reform that would be made for the next several years.

John McCain, the senator from Arizona and 2008 Republican candidate for the presidency, would shift his positions radically as he tried to please party hard-liners. He had been a true leader, championing, along with Kennedy, the cause of comprehensive immigration reform. But bowing to mounting pressures from the conservative base of the Republican Party as he fought for their nomination, he did an about-face and publicly adopted their iso-lationist views, opposing any legislative initiative that would seem to favor undocumented immigrants or hold out any possibility of a path to citizenship.

During a televised debate among the Republican candidates for the presidential nomination in January 2008, McCain sur-prised everyone by lambasting himself for ever having tried to reform the immigration system, stating that "today I would not

vote for that reform." McCain abruptly toed the party line, trying to reassure his party's overwhelmingly white base that: "First
of all, we need to secure the borders and deport all the illegals."[2]

For his part, candidate Obama issued a bold promise: to pass
immigration reform within the first year of his administration.
He would present such legislation within the first three months
of his inauguration, he vowed. In his zeal to set himself apart
from Hillary Clinton, who supported immigration reform efforts
but had expressed opposition to issuing drivers licenses for unauthorized immigrants, Obama announced his support for allowing
undocumented immigrants to have driver's licenses at a debate of
the Democratic primary candidates in Las Vegas. Obama was desperate to get the Latino vote and the driver's license issue proved
to be a moot point, because the documents are issued by the states
with no input from the federal government and Obama never
mentioned it again during his campaign or so far during the first
term of his presidency.

If the fastest-growing segment of voters in the country—
Latinos—did not overcome their reluctance to support him, a
man they didn't know and who didn't have a substantial legislative record or high profile, Obama could not have eventually
become president. Obama's promise to enact immigration reform
was rash and probably cynical; at a time when the country's economy was imploding and in the wake of the spectacular failure of
the 2006 attempt at legislative reform, it would be extremely difficult for a new president to fulfill. But Obama told Latino voters
that the only chance they could have at real reform would be with
a Democratic president, with two Democratic-majority houses of
Congress. On May 28, 2008, then candidate Barack Obama had
told Jorge Ramos, the most important journalist on the biggest
Spanish network in the country: "I can guarantee that during the
first year of my term, we will have an immigration reform package

[in Congress] which I will vigorously support, and will personally promote. And I want to do this as quickly as possible."[3]

In November 2008, 67 percent of Latino voters cast their ballots for Obama and helped to deliver both chambers of Congress to the Democratic Party. Yet the initiative for reforming immigration laws that was supposed to have been presented to Congress with sponsors from both parties and fully supported by his administration—exactly what Obama had committed to on more than one occasion during the campaign, especially to the Spanish-language news media—never materialized.

Over the next few years, Obama made a few speeches in favor of immigration reform to various audiences, yet the actions of his administration were, at least during the first three years of his administration, diametrically opposed to the content of his speeches.

By the summer of 2011, three years after the supposed president for change took power, pro-immigrant groups around the country were at war with the actions of his government. Obama and his Department of Homeland Security (DHS), headed by Janet Napolitano, clearly had maintained two separate dialogues on immigration. The dialogues seemingly were meant to satisfy everyone but actually did not politically satisfy anyone.

Like so many of the measures taken over the previous twenty years, many of those taken between 2009 and 2011 were meant to placate one political sector or another—generally the one arguing that immigrants are doing the country much more harm than good. But the measures had very little impact on the real issue: the immigration system that for decades has been completely out of sync with the economic needs of the country and with the philosophical, moral, and social principles on which the nation was founded. Today the immigration system, like the banking system—two pillars of the most powerful economy in the world—does not function for the good of the nation as a whole but for a few powerful beneficiaries. But reforming either system would exact a political price that no one, it seems, is willing to pay.

BROKEN PROMISES

When Obama took office in 2009, his first important decision was choosing the head of the DHS, who would oversee the country's immigration policies. The various federal immigration agencies, border control, customs, and similar functions all fall under this department, ever since the reorganization that took place following the events of September 11, 2001. Since that time, immigration has been an issue contained under the umbrella of law enforcement and national security.

President Obama selected Janet Napolitano for this powerful office. Napolitano was the governor of Arizona from 2003 to 2009 and the state's attorney general from 1999 to 2002. Her track record did not give a clear impression of what side of the debate she would come down on in her new role or which direction would best advance her own political ambitions.

As Arizona's attorney general, Napolitano had forged an unorthodox alliance with the controversial and popular Maricopa County sheriff Joe Arpaio. Arpaio had gained notoriety in the mid-1990s for making the prisoners in his jails eat green bologna and wear pink underwear, allegedly to degrade and humiliate them. He is now well known for devoting the resources of his office to capture and deport undocumented immigrants above all other priorities.

As sheriff of Maricopa County, which includes the capital city of Phoenix, Arpaio and his police department are responsible for law enforcement in parts of the county that are not officially part of a municipality or that don't have their own police departments. And his department processes prisoners, administers the region's jails, and arrests those suspected of breaking the law.

In recent years, Arpaio has focused most of his resources on his notorious immigrant roundups, searching for undocumented people to arrest and hand over to federal authorities. The inmates in pink underwear housed in the tents that Arpaio introduced after the jails were filled to capacity were mainly undocumented immigrants who had been caught in raids or stopped for minor traffic violations. Arpaio, who has never met a television camera he doesn't like, reached new levels of popularity as the "toughest sheriff in the country."

By the mid-1990s, his critics charged that the conditions in Arpaio's jails represented a clear human rights violation. After the death of a prisoner, the DOJ ordered an investigation into the tent cities Arpaio had instituted, and the US Attorney appointed to lead the investigation was Janet Napolitano.

Napolitano, who at the time had her eyes on the governor's office, conducted the investigation. Two years later, she produced a report that concluded that the conditions in the prisons were a disaster; excessive force was used on the inmates; personnel were insufficient "to guarantee the most minimal security and humane operation" of the prisons; and pepper spray and restraint chairs were overused. (When a prisoner is placed in a restraint chair, his arms, legs, and torso are tied to the chair. It has been condemned by critics as a form of torture, and its use has resulted in several deaths in jails across the country.[4])

The DOJ reached an agreement with Arpaio after he agreed to make "administrative changes," although immediately thereafter the sheriff told the *Arizona Republic* that "the prisoners will continue to be chained and wear pink underwear. This whole investigation has nothing to do with my programs to protect the people of Maricopa."[5]

In 2002, when Napolitano was the Democratic candidate for governor, Arpaio, a member of the Republican Party, appeared in a television commercial singing her praises. She won the election by a very narrow margin—by less than 1 percent of the votes—and Arpaio's support may have been what pushed her over the edge to victory. The Republican candidate, Matt Salmon, had asked for Arpaio's support but had been rebuffed. The strange political alliance between the sheriff and the attorney who had investigated him led to a great deal of speculation.

A few years later, the new governor and Arpaio clashed when the renegade operations of the "toughest sheriff in the West" became increasingly more difficult to justify. In 2008, the Goldwater Institute, an organization with ties to Arizona conservative groups, concluded that while the sheriff sent out officers to arrest undocumented immigrants during traffic stops, thousands of arrest warrants for serious crimes went unprocessed; a high percentage of investigations carried out by Arpaio's department went nowhere; and the county had to settle lawsuits demanding millions of dollars because of the sheriff's excesses.

"Although MCSO [Maricopa County Sheriff's Office] is adept at self-promotion and is an unquestionably 'tough' law-enforcement agency, under its watch violent crime rates recently have soared, both in absolute terms and relative to other jurisdictions," the Goldwater Institute reported in December 2008. "It has diverted resources away from basic law-enforcement functions to highly publicized immigration sweeps, which are ineffective in policing illegal immigration and in reducing crime generally."[6]

The relationship between Arpaio and Napolitano continued to be more or less contentious, especially after Arpaio let his own aspirations for the governor's office be known—between immigrations sweeps and book signings.

On January 20, 2009, Napolitano was confirmed as the Obama administration's secretary of Homeland Security. Jan Brewer stepped into the governor's office in Arizona and would later become a hero of the anti-immigrant movement when she signed into law SB 1070.

Barack Obama's government and the new secretary of Homeland Security got to work to overhaul and streamline the system in place for capturing and deporting undocumented people. If immigration had been one of the Obama's top priorities during his campaign, upon taking office, his priorities shifted: The focus became application and swift execution of the deportation laws and penalties for the undocumented already on the books but only intermittently applied until then.

The hard line that the Obama administration took surprised many of the president's supporters and fellow Democrats. One of the first changes enacted was suspending raids on businesses to arrest undocumented workers and focusing instead on employer audits, checking the employee paperwork of companies and subcontractors.

Obama had been a critic of the spectacular workplace raids carried out by George W. Bush in the last two years of his second term. In the raids, federal agents descended on factories and businesses with no warning, hunting for undocumented workers, often arresting dozens and, in a few cases, hundreds of workers on the spot.

One of the most notorious instances was the raid on the meat-processing company Swift that took place in December 2006 in six states. Going after this kind of plant, where the workers perform extremely difficult, dirty, and relatively poorly paid jobs, is like shaking low-hanging fruit from a tree: Everything that falls is profit. Almost thirteen hundred people were arrested. Many were charged with identity theft for using false social security numbers, a tactic increasingly used by federal authorities in the last ten years to attach a serious crime to the charge of working illegally, even though these immigrants were using their supposed stolen identities only for the privilege of toiling away at the meat-packing plant and not, say, to rack up charges on credit cards in someone else's name.

"I think these raids are a show that doesn't solve the problem," Barack Obama said to this reporter during an interview in
the spring of 2008. "We have 12 million undocumented immigrants; the idea that we can solve that by arresting fifty here and
there is dishonest. And I'm not interested in making it a priority
to arrest workers trying to support their families. I want there to
be a path to citizenship for immigrants."[7]

Analyzing his comments with the benefit of hindsight, I wonder if Obama was playing with words: Was he trying to say the
raids should be stopped because they were inhumane or because
there were more effective ways to deport larger numbers of people
more quickly?

Putting a stop to the workplace raids was a promise Obama
did keep, although his administration started a new strategy of
conducting worker file audits that were dubbed "paper raids."
The new, aggressive strategy requires thousands of companies to
open their books to verify the eligibility of their workers for legal
employment, with a special focus on "the most serious infractions
of the labor laws," such as a company having a large number of
unauthorized workers on payroll.

If hiring undocumented workers is advantageous to businesses
because they can pay them lower wages, because workers without
papers have fewer job options and are afraid of being reported
to authorities and therefore easy to exploit, the intelligent thing
to do is to punish employers, so that the cost of hiring undocumented workers exceeds the benefits of breaking the law.

The numbers the government reported on its own efforts are
impressive at first glance: By October 2010, the Obama administration audited 3,200 employers, shut down 225 companies or
business owners, and imposed fines and penalties totaling $50
million. It also filed charges against 196 employers.[8]

In early 2011, the DHS announced that another 1,000 employers would be audited, while Republican hard-liners in Congress,

including Lamar Smith (Texas), Elton Gallegly (California), and Steve King (Iowa), citing high unemployment and the recession, pushed for the obligatory use of the E-Verify system, although its high margins of error due to an unreliable database are well known.

"With 26 million Americans unemployed or underemployed, expanding E-Verify would help to open up jobs they need," Smith said before a congressional committee in February 2011.[9]

In the absence of comprehensive immigration reform, neither auditing employers nor E-Verify seems destined to solve the problem of an immigration system that has not been evaluated meaningfully since 1965. What does seem to be happening is that those measures will cause businesses, workers, and the country as a whole to suffer without producing significant positive results.

As mentioned, auditing companies seems to be a much more efficient tactic than raids on workplaces resulting in the deportations of some workers in a poultry plant or textile factory. But the numbers speak for themselves: There are over 7 million employers in the United States and 150 million workers in the workforce, of whom 8 million may be undocumented (5.3 percent). ICE has only 522 agents dedicated to workplace enforcement.[10]

Progress in the area of immigration enforcement is slow, and the final proof of the effectiveness of the approach will be the significant reduction of the number of undocumented people in the United States. The theory is that with no jobs to be had, foreigners without legal permission to work will pack up and go home. According to various studies, in spite of the recession, there are no signs that that is happening as of this writing.

On the contrary: Despite the stepped-up pace of deportations, employer sanctions, and increased border security over the past fourteen years, at a cost of almost $11 billion for Customs and Border Protection, $6 billion for ICE, millions of dollars for the expansion of detention centers for immigrants, and more prison space for the growing list of obligatory detainments required by increasingly strict immigration laws enacted since 1995, according to every major research institute studying the issue, there have been no significant changes in the numbers of undocumented immigrants in the country.

The Pew Center's 2011 estimates of the undocumented population indicated there were 1 million fewer undocumented people than there were in 2007, at the beginning of the financial crisis. According to recent studies, the recession has resulted in a significant drop in the number of immigrants crossing the Mexican border.[11] But the immigrants already in the United States are not returning to their countries of origin, where the situation is even worse. Also, their families and lives in general are now firmly based here. Most of those who are no longer here have left because they were deported, but, nevertheless, the overall number of undocumented people has been virtually unchanged in the last few years.[12]

As far as the E-Verify program goes, many significant adjustments would have to be made in order for the system to function as Smith, Gallegly, and King think it should. But the congressmen seem satisfied with simply invoking the program to placate their political base rather than using it to solve a real problem. If they really wanted to eliminate what is attracting undocumented immigrants to this country in the first place, how can they explain their insistence on using the E-Verify program, which, according to the government's own studies, does not detect identity theft or the unauthorized use of legitimate social security numbers?[13] E-Verify only determines whether a social security number is legitimate or fabricated, and many numbers undocumented immigrants buy in order to obtain work papers are in fact authentic but have been stolen by identity theft rings.

And as journalist and National Public Radio commentator Rubén Navarrette pointed out on May 29, 2011, E-Verify does not apply to "the one group that employs most illegal immigrants: American homeowners."[14] Such people hire, for a bargain price and under the table, immigrants as housecleaners, nannies, gardeners, handymen, painters, and for other jobs that make the lives of middle- and upper-class Americans run smoothly.

At a time when the United States was experiencing the worst recession since the Great Depression and when approval ratings for Congress had plummeted to the lowest levels ever (11 percent, according to a January 2012 CNN poll[15]), legislators and the White House insisted that the entire immigration problem could be solved by penalizing a tiny percentage of employers and identifying a small number of unauthorized workers. And the cost of implementing those modest measures would reach spectacular levels.

And, as Navarrette also pointed out, the tired argument used by Smith and other politicians that undocumented workers "take jobs away" from Americans is questionable at best: "How many Americans do you know who complain that it was their life's dream to pick strawberries, or tar roofs, or clean horse stalls, or do some other hard and dirty job but, darn it, an illegal immigrant got there first?" asks Navarrette, a journalist known for his conservative leanings.

The only job creation plans many congressional representatives can come up with consist of cutting taxes for employers and getting rid of illegal immigrants, most of whom perform the jobs at the very lowest rungs of the workforce ladder while also contributing to the economy by creating jobs in their communities—they generate other economic activities, pay taxes, and consume goods.

Some analysts point out the absurdity of trying to control the flow of workers in a marketplace where capital is free to cross borders and companies are free to take their factories and businesses—and the jobs with them—somewhere else. The irony is that the politicians who espouse completely free markets with minimal government intervention into business practices want to aggressively and intrusively control the labor force those businesses most need. This stance defies logical explanation. The ideologies touted by anti-immigrant conservatives are not based on economic truths or the broader reality of the country but purely on politics and a kind of populist public discourse that allows the status quo to stay intact. The current system of legal immigration does not work for the economy of the country, but its consequence—illegal immigration—serves to inspire enough attention-grabbing slogans to appeal to voters and ensure politicians' continued employment at their own jobs.

DEPORTATIONS FULL SPEED AHEAD

Under Barack Obama's administration, the ICE became a highly efficient deportation machine, much more so than it had ever been under George W. Bush. And Obama never supported or presented a package for immigration reform to Congress, as Bush had done in 2006–2007. In fact, immigration reform was never a top priority during Obama's first term, despite his campaign promises. How could it have been? With a full plate of issues ranging from the financial crisis, the promise of getting the troops out of Iraq and the pledge to "win" in Afghanistan, and the decision to reform the health care system, immigration was placed on the back burner.

For most of the first two years of his administration, Obama's close political advisor and chief of staff was Rahm Emmanuel, who was vehemently opposed to dealing with immigration reform. He told Hispanic leaders that attempting immigration reform would be possible only during Obama's second term in office.[16] Emmanuel generally has been seen as having the most decisive influence on the president, and in large part responsible for the non-fulfillment of the calculated promise that President Obama had made to immigrants when he was running for the job.

At the same time, and as tends to happen with Democratic presidents, the movement toward reform first had to cleanse itself by putting in place the most conservative measures possible first and proving the president's good intentions within the context of Republican priorities: "enforcement first." As *La Opinión* Washington-based correspondent Maribel Hastings observed, what happened after Obama took office was "a surge in policies that have resulted in more deportations—among other things—all designed to clear the way for an immigration reform, the very idea of which, in any case, scares politicians away like the Devil fleeing from the cross."[17]

Among the more controversial measures perfected by ICE under Obama was one initially approved in 1996 by Bill Clinton, the other Democratic president who promoted the "enforcement first" concept almost before the Republicans had invented it. The Illegal Immigration Reform and Immigrant Responsibility Act of 1996 added Section 287(g) to the Immigration and Nationality Act, authorizing the federal government to enter into agreements with local police departments and train the officers in immigration enforcement. Under the supervision of ICE agents, police received training and were then allowed to enforce federal immigration laws during the course of their routine work.

A few years later, the program dubbed "Secure Communities," initially created by the Bush administration but greatly expanded in 2009 under the new director of ICE, John Morton, deliberately erased the dividing line drawn between local police and immigration authorities. According to many legal experts, breaking that line could mean jeopardizing public safety in states and cities with high immigrant populations.

Secure Communities was established as a pilot program in some prisons to process the digital fingerprints of detainees and run them through federal databases, including immigration, to discover if the person was undocumented. Unlike 287(g), this program did not require any special agreements between the federal government and local law enforcement. During the first three years of the Obama administration, it was implemented virtually nationwide. Contrary to the stated aims of the program, most of the detainees who were deported as a result were not dangerous "criminals" but people without any prior criminal record who had been detained for some minor infraction, such as driving without a license or, say, selling ice cream on the street without a vendor's license.[18]

According to some analysts, these programs had another effect: discouraging undocumented immigrants from cooperating with the police in any way, such as by reporting a crime or helping with an investigation into a crime within their communities.

The case of Abel Moreno, an undocumented immigrant living in Charlotte, North Carolina, attracted a great deal of attention in early 2011 for exemplifying the danger posed to the public by combining local police work and immigration enforcement. "Just like the police tell you to do, Abel Moreno called 911 when a man began assaulting his girlfriend," reported an article on NBC's website. The man groping his girlfriend was a police officer who had pulled them over. When he saw Moreno making the call, he arrested them both, charging them with resisting arrest.

After that incident, five other women came forward and reported that the same officer had tried to sexually assault them. The officer was investigated, and Moreno was a key witness. But when he had been taken into police custody for "resisting arrest," he was identified as an illegal immigrant under the Secure Communities program and faced possible deportation to Mexico, even though the Mecklenburg County Sheriff's Office acknowledges that he should never have been arrested in the first place. He also lost his job at a local restaurant.

The media have reported many cases similar to Moreno's. For undocumented immigrants, the message is clear: The less contact they have with the police, the better, even if that means failing to report a crime perpetrated against themselves or anyone else.

Moreno's case has a happy ending: He was eventually granted a U Visa, a special class of visas for victims or witnesses to crimes who are willing to cooperate with the authorities, that would allow him to apply for permanent residency after four years. All the publicity his case received may have helped. But the overall result of 287(g) and Secure Communities is that any undocumented person who comes into contact with the local police for any reason could wind up being deported. In a few instances, even US citizens have been deported because of errors in the system.[19]

The Obama administration aggressively employed both federal programs to reach record numbers of deportation: 1.2 million people were deported in the first two years of his administration.[20] Since 2008, the DHS has expanded Secure Communities from just fourteen jurisdictions to over thirteen hundred in only three years.

But the more the Secure Communities program grew, the more opposition it generated—not just from pro-immigrant activist groups but from other groups much less willing to overlook any infractions of law: the police themselves and chiefs of police. Secure Communities was especially controversial because, according to the government's own data, at least 50 percent of those deported were not criminals but simply workers, many of them with families to support.[21] As mentioned, in some widely publicized cases, they were themselves crime victims who had stepped forward to make a complaint. At the heart of the controversy is the way in which the program functions, by linking the work of routine community policing with the identification of people eligible for deportation.

In practice, under Secure Communities, the biometric data of every person arrested or detained for any reason, no matter how minor the alleged infraction or whether they are released without charges, are sent from local jails to federal databases of the Federal Bureau of Identification, Automated Biometric Identification System (IDENT), and US-VISIT. With that information, authorities can immediately determine whether a person is undocumented or has any action pending for violating immigration laws. ICE does not have the resources to deport everyone—it is estimated that it costs taxpayers $23,000 to deport one immigrant—so it evaluates cases and decides who will be subjected to the deportation process, based on certain criteria.

The explicit promise of the Obama administration was to make deporting dangerous criminals the top priority. But this was easier said than done. At the time of this writing, only 15 percent of those deported under the Secure Communities program are foreigners charged with a class 1 felony, a category that includes those accused—not just those convicted—of crimes that carry a minimum sentence of one year in prison. This approach turns the "innocent until proven guilty" principle of our justice system on its head.

"It's not clear how ICE is ensuring that the program focuses on the most dangerous criminals that pose a threat to public safety," observes Brittney Nystrom, an attorney with the National Immigration Forum in Washington, DC. "It's not even applied to suspects that have been convicted, but when they've been arrested."[22]

According to ICE's own data, through October 31, 2011, 110,000 "foreign criminals" had been deported, and of those 39,500 were convicted of felony (level 1) crimes[23]—35 percent of the overall number of "criminals." So 65 percent of the foreign criminals deported were not in the "serious felon" category, which, according to ICE director John Morton, was what the Secure Communities program would focus on.

ICE's own data shows that roughly half of those who were eventually deported were not charged with any crime as a result of their initial arrest or were charged with a misdemeanor offense. Local law enforcement insists that the arrest and deportation of such individuals poses a serious challenge for their work guaranteeing public safety in the larger community.

"To us, the people responsible for maintaining order, it seems that this program should be used to go after dangerous criminals who are here illegally, not people who drive without a license—because you can't get one if you're undocumented—or because they were drinking a beer in someone's doorway," San Francisco sheriff Mike Hennessey told a local paper. "When the local police are required to enforce immigration laws, the trust between the local community and the authorities is broken."[24]

Complaints about the program continued to mount. On June 10, 2011, a group of congressional representatives from southern California held a press conference on the steps of City Hall in Los Angeles, urging Governor Jerry Brown to suspend his state's participation in the program.[25] "We have the case of Maria, twenty-one years old, who was beaten by her boyfriend and when the police arrived, they were both arrested. Once in custody, she was reported to the immigration authorities and deported. Her two-year-old daughter stayed here, growing up without her mother," Congresswoman Lucille Roybal Allard of Los Angeles said. "And there's the single mother of three children in Hayworth, California, who was deported after a car accident. In times of crisis, I don't see the point of going after men and women who are just trying to support their families. We should be deporting the real criminals."[26]

During the summer of 2011, public forums were held to study the program after months of complaints and protests from communities, police departments, and even state governments. At these meetings, many stories were told of undocumented people who had gotten swept up by the Secure Communities program after voluntarily going to the police to report a crime.

The program generated such controversy that three state governments decided to opt out of it entirely: Illinois, Massachusetts, and New York. In his letter to Janet Napolitano, Governor Andrew Cuomo of New York explained, "Secure Communities has exactly the opposite of the intended effect. Its intention is to catch those who represent a serious threat to public safety, but it compromises public safety by discouraging witnesses to crimes and other members of the community from cooperating with authorities."[27]

There is wide suspicion that some police departments are stopping people based on aspects of their physical appearance, such as the color of their skin—which constitutes racial profiling and is unconstitutional—and even based on what kind of clothes and shoes they wear. Republican California congressman and chair of the anti-immigration Immigration Reform Caucus Brian Bilbray recommended on MSNBC's *Hardball with Chris Matthews,* aired on June 22, 2010, that to identify undocumented immigrants the police could " . . . look at the kind of dress you wear, there is different type of attire, there is different type of—right down to the shoes, right down to the clothes."

Sacramento's former chief of police Arturo Venegas has said that "there are police all over the country who are arresting and processing people based on their appearance, knowing full well that even if they are released without any criminal charge, they will be caught by immigration authorities."[28] Evidence of flagrantly unconstitutional activity prompted the inspector general of the DHS to open a high-level investigation into the Secure Communities program in May 2011. Meanwhile, the Obama administration has indicated that it intends to "improve the record of arresting criminals" while doggedly pursuing its unstated goal of breaking all deportation records.[29]

FOURTEEN
THE REPUBLICANS
STUCK ON IMMIGRATION

AT THE END OF SEPTEMBER 2011, DURING A DEBATE OF THE REPUBLICAN CANdidates for the presidential nomination, Texas governor Rick Perry did the unthinkable: He tried to argue in favor of providing an education for young undocumented immigrants who wanted to go to college.

"If you say that we should not educate children who have come into our state for no other reason than they have been brought there by no fault of their own, I don't think you have a heart," he said at the Fox News debate. "We need to be educating these children because they will become a drag on our society."[1]

At the time, Perry was the man to beat, the great hope of the conservatives, the governor of a state that understood Latino issues better than any other. He had a good track record for creating jobs and improving the state's economy, important at a time when jobs and the economy surely would be the dominant themes of the upcoming presidential race.

Perry also asserted that trying to build a wall along the border was not a practical solution. "Have you ever even been to the border with Mexico?" Perry challenged Rick Santorum, the former senator from Pennsylvania, at the debate. "The idea that you are going to build a wall, a fence for 1,200 miles, and then go

800 miles more to Tijuana, does not make sense." Like Ronald Reagan before him, Perry was not in favor of a border fence.

In that same debate, Santorum called Perry "soft" on illegal immigration, even softer than Barack Obama. Mitt Romney, the former governor of Massachusetts, said that Perry's statement "doesn't make any sense to me." Congressman Ron Paul (R-TX) stated: "What you need to do is attack their benefits: no free education, no free subsidies, no citizenship, no birthright citizenship." Former Utah Governor Jon Huntsman remarked: "For Rick to say ya can't secure the border is pretty much a treasonous comment."

Instead of describing them as not having a heart, Perry could have said it seemed like his Republican rivals were not using their brains. Characterizing his opponents as not having a heart on this issue was the weakest argument he could have made. Being against allowing young undocumented immigrants who had lived in the United States for most of their lives and who were academically qualified for college from advancing in their studies is not just cruel; rather, it represents a stunning lack of vision regarding the economic future of this country.

But reason does not apparently play a role in political discussions on many subjects, immigration being one of the most prominent. Emotions and the views of a hardened anti-immigrant minority on laws they consider to be unchangeable seem to be more relevant.

The United States is facing an imminent shortage of highly qualified professionals in science, technology, engineering, and health care. According to estimates from Georgetown University, by 2018—right around the corner—there will be a shortage of approximately 3 million professionals.[2] Two-thirds of those vacant positions require advanced university degrees. Nevertheless, cuts in education spending at the college and university level all across the country, and the deficient foundation that so many students receive in math and sciences in the elementary and high school grades, means that it will become increasingly difficult to fill positions so essential to our economy.

Another perhaps less important but equally powerful argument is that, in poll after poll, a clear majority of Americans have declared their support for the DREAM Act, which would allow these young students to obtain legal status in addition to pursuing a higher education (or military service).[3] But these facts did not affect the tone of the discussion during the campaign for the Republican nomination. Much more was said about not rewarding "illegal" activity, even though the vast majority of young people without status were brought here as young children or infants and in no way participated knowingly in any illegal act.

In terms of US politics in general and election-year politics in particular, immigration is an extremely controversial topic. Politicians in particular, especially in the Republican Party, seem to have a blind spot when it comes to this issue.

New York mayor Michael Bloomberg, a former Republican turned independent, and Michigan governor Rick Snyder, a Republican, explained the phenomenon in an op-ed piece published in February 2012 in newspapers across the country. "The trouble is that the debate around immigration is too often focused on politics, not economics," they point out.

That was certainly the case in the Republican primary contest in 2011 and 2012. Over the long months of campaigning, the subject of immigration came up many times, but not one candidate offered a concrete plan for instituting a coherent immigration policy. The candidates mostly tap-danced to placate the most conservative elements of the party and those most reflexively opposed to considering any solution that would mean integrating any undocumented immigrants already in the country into our society.

Under vociferous attack from his rivals, Perry not only had to apologize for what he had said, but he eventually abandoned his position altogether. And even though his "without a heart" comment was not the principal problem with his campaign, that event marked the first time in the 2012 campaign that a Republican hopeful would dare to deviate from party orthodoxy on the question of what to do with the millions of undocumented people within the United States and the future of the immigration system.

Other candidates had more success, at least in the short term, invoking heavy-handed solutions sure to appeal to their base. Michelle Bachmann, the congresswoman from Minnesota affiliated with the Tea Party, said the answer was to make English the country's official language and to construct not just one wall but a double wall along the border, making it impossible to enter the country illegally.

The most provocative solution was offered by Herman Cain, the pizza impresario who briefly led the Republican field for the nomination. During a Tea Party event in Tennessee in October 2011, Cain outlined his plan for preventing illegal border crossings.

"We'll have a real fence, twenty feet high, with barbed wire, electrified, with a sign on the other side that says, 'It can kill you,'" Cain said, to raucous applause from the crowd. "What do you mean, *insensitive?* What is insensitive is when they come to the United States across our border and kill our citizens and kill our border-patrol people."[4]

The following day, Cain explained that his statement, which had been delivered straight-faced and with righteous indignation, had been "a joke." He added, "America needs to get a sense of humor."

Immigration was not what sank the presidential hopes of Bachman, Huntsman, Cain, or even Perry, but their campaigns offered few good ideas for how to solve the immigration problem. This particular contest can be viewed as a microcosm of how politics prevents the United States from seeking real solutions to the dynamics of illegal immigration and the deficiencies in the legal immigration system that foment it.

Immigration is not a high-priority issue for most Republican voters, who are more concerned with government spending, the national debt, the deficit, the effects of the health care reform legislation, and their collective disdain for Barack Obama's performance as president. During the primary, when the subject was raised in the race for the presidential nomination, Republican hopefuls took the surest path: always invoking restrictive measures, the supremacy of the law, and the supposed benefits of deportation.

Almost all the attention the issue has received during the primary campaign among Republicans has focused on the existence of illegal or undocumented immigrants and especially their negative impact. Little or no attention has been paid to the carefully thought out views of academics and business leaders who are sounding the alarm on the overly complex legal immigration system and the urgent necessity to reform it.

But when the question has arisen on what to do with all of the undocumented immigrations, the solutions proposed have been overly political and simplistic.

Mitt Romney is a special case. From the beginning of his campaign for the presidential nomination, he sought to protect his right flank at all times, threatened as he was by the Tea Party activists and conservatives of all stripes, who remembered all the flip-flops he has made over the years on political issues that are very important to them. For example, Romney supported comprehensive immigration reform when it was discussed in Congress in 2006 and 2007. But in 2008, during his first presidential campaign, he pared down his ideas on reform to simply "avoid amnesty and protect the borders." In 2011, Romney memorably aligned himself with Kris Kobach, the ideologue behind the concept of self-deportation.

This concept, explained in more detail in chapter 9, became part of Mitt Romney's plan to solve the problem of undocumented immigration. It basically means undocumented immigrants will voluntarily leave (deport themselves) because they can't find work, to escape relentless persecution by authorities, and to rejoin their families. According to Kobach and other advocates, self-deportation would be the natural result of the vigorous application of severe immigration laws passed on the state level in Alabama, Arizona, Georgia, and others, which would empower any police officer and even any citizen to enforce federal immigration law.

In an interview published in February 2012, Kobach said he and Romney had discussed the possibility of applying these kinds of measures to the entire country, if Romney made it to the White House.[5] According to Kobach, that would result in a mass exodus of 5.5 million people, almost half of the total number of undocumented people in the United States.

"You could reasonably expect that in the first four years a new administration, if attrition through enforcement were made the central centerpiece of national immigration policy, you could see the illegal alien population cut in half," Kobach said.

The Romney campaign did not deny his connection with Kobach, although the candidate has not always explicitly mentioned the plan in his statements about immigration. Another seemingly contradictory idea Romney has talked about is giving undocumented immigrants temporary worker visas and eliminating the jobs magnet so that would-be undocumented immigrants would know that they cannot come here to work without official status.

Theoretically, the use of E-Verify, employer sanctions, and the laws resulting in self-deportation would do the rest: With the wave of a magic wand, millions of people would disappear—people who have started families here with children who are US citizens, people with businesses, homes, and other deep roots in this country.

In December 2011, at an event in Iowa, Romney explained: "We're not going to go across the country and round people up. It's just too big of a task. There are what? Eleven, twelve, fifteen million—who knows the total number? But what we are going to do is we are going to give people a chance to transition to be able to go home to get in line and then, ultimately if they would like to, to have a green card to come into this country legally."[6]

The orderly line Romney alludes to means waits of up to twenty years for entry into the United States from certain countries, such as Mexico and the Philippines, and several years from many other countries. Aside from that reality, if current law remains unchanged, people who have lived in the United States without legal documentation are barred from reentering the country for a minimum of five and as long as ten years.

Romney and the other Republican hopefuls did not have much discussion about how the legal immigration system should be reformed, even if they were in favor of doing so. Romney's close relationship with Kobach and his allies at the Federation for American Immigration Reform, an organization whose ultimate goal is to reduce *legal* immigration, makes it hard to predict which side he would come down on when the time comes to tackle comprehensive reform.

Another relevant topic that has not been discussed is the effects the direct or indirect expulsion of so many millions of people will have on the economy. If the exodus of a few thousand undocumented workers could have such a serious impact on the agricultural and local economies in Georgia and Alabama (where crops rotted in the fields during 2011) after the passage of local laws, it is reasonable to believe that driving out 5 or 7 or 9 million people would have national consequences.

This population of undocumented people is not a special, isolated group living in a vacuum whose expulsion would affect the country only in positive ways. We are talking about 11 million people, two-thirds of whom have lived in this country for over ten years, according to the Pew Research Center, and 73 percent of whom have children who are American citizens.[7]

At a debate in November 2011, to the great surprise of his rivals, Newt Gingrich, former Speaker of the House and would-be presidential nominee, suggested that "something" had to be done about those millions of people beyond simply underscoring that their illegality makes them disposable, the view expressed by most candidates in the context of the Republican primaries until that time, with the exception of Rick Perry in the previously mentioned debate. At another televised discussion in Washington DC, Gingrich said, "I don't see how the party that says it's the party of the family is going to adopt an immigration policy which destroys families which have been here a quarter-century. And I am prepared to take the heat for saying, let's be humane in enforcing the law without giving them citizenship, but finding a way to give them legality as not to separate them from their families."[8]

But at the ABC News Iowa Republican debate the following month, Gingrich affirmed that his plan would apply only to undocumented immigrants who had been in the United States for at least twenty-five years. Moderator Diane Sawyer pressed for specifics, saying, "But the Pew Center for Hispanic Research has said maybe 3.5 million people could come under the criteria that you laid out . . . who have been here fifteen years." Gingrich countered: "You used a number that doesn't relate to my proposal. . . . The person has to have been here twenty-five years . . . and they still don't get citizenship. This is not amnesty. They get residency. And they pay a penalty in order to get residency."[9]

There is no precise estimate of how many undocumented immigrants have lived here for at least twenty-five years. But it's likely the figure would represent only a small fraction of the 3.5 million who have been here for over fifteen years, since most undocumented immigrants currently in the country arrived in the 1990s and later. Twenty-five years ago takes us back to 1986, the year Ronald Reagan's Immigration Reform and Control Act—the Amnesty Law—went into effect, granting legal status to undocumented immigrants who had been in the country since before 1982. Assuming that at least half of those 3.5 million people have been here for twenty-five years, Gingrich's "legalization" plan would benefit fewer than 2 million people.

"The universe of people who could qualify is very small and the benefits they receive are unclear," said a report by the Center for American Progress (CAP), a group based in Washington, DC. "Gingrich envisions the creation of committees of citizen review that would make decisions about who deserves legal status. The few people who qualify will be prohibited from applying for U.S. citizenship or receiv[ing] federal benefits."[10]

Gingrich's plan was the most specific plan that the Republican candidates offered during the primary campaign, but the conditions restrict the numbers of people who could meet all of the requirements. For example, in order to obtain the type of noncitizen legal residence Gingrich imagines, applicants would have to prove that they can afford private health insurance and maintain that eligibility, or risk losing their legal status and pay a fine of $5,000. "That alone would disqualify many Americans," the CAP report points out. "Even for those who qualify, this is a program of high risk and low rewards."

Gingrich took what he believes to be the most politically expedient course of action: advocating for some kind of solution, no matter how limited it may be, while also avoiding an outcome that apparently strikes fear into the hearts of many Republicans: allowing millions of undocumented immigrants to eventually become citizens and join the Democratic Party.

"We are not going to deport people who have been here for a very long time and who have deep family ties," Gingrich said in an interview with this author in Los Angeles,[11] "We have to find the middle ground, the country is not going to give them amnesty, so it's better to offer residency without citizenship."

Gingrich proposes a state of permanent internal exile: No matter how long people have lived in the United States, they will never have any chance to fully integrate into the country's political life. Nevertheless, as of this writing, this proposal is the best one any Republican presidential hopeful has made on how to integrate 11 million undocumented immigrants into the country and reform the immigration system.[12]

FIFTEEN
THE ECONOMY, IMMIGRANTS, AND THE FUTURE OF AMERICA

In the unforgiving global economy of the 21st century, employment-based immigration represents a strategic resource. If managed well, immigration can actively support economic growth and competitiveness while protecting U.S. workers' wages and working conditions.

—Demetrios Papademetriou, president of
the Migration Policy Institute

DURING A RECESSION, QUESTIONS INEVITABLY ARISE ABOUT WHAT EFFECT IMmigrants, especially undocumented or illegal immigrants, have on the rest of the population, the economy in general, and the US treasury.

The overriding concerns seem to be rooted in the country's reality: When unemployment levels are high, it's assumed that the blame rests largely with illegal immigrants, who unlawfully take jobs they have no right to, working for lower wages and presumably not paying their fair share of taxes.

Many politicians have a quick and easy solution to this problem, and it's often the only economic plan they offer: Get rid of those immigrants, deport them, throw them in prison, pass laws against them so they are pressured to "self-deport"—problem solved.

In the collective imagination, illegal immigrants are job stealers who don't pay taxes and are a burden for people who do. At least that's the stock argument of those who believe undocumented immigrants are nothing more than a dead weight dragging down the country that unwillingly hosts them. What follows is, naturally, a call for more and better methods of expulsion and deportation, which would solve the problem and free up jobs for deserving citizens.

The issue is more complex than it seems on its face, since according to wide research on the subject, the effects undocumented immigrants have on the economy depend on many variables: the specific industries they work in, the historical context, the laws in place, and the country's economic needs at the time.

Drawing a purely negative conclusion would be just as inaccurate as coming to a purely positive one. Undocumented immigrants make important contributions to the economy as a whole by working in industries where the United States no longer has a sufficient workforce of its own to draw on. Agriculture is a typical example, but there are other sectors as well, some of which will become increasingly important in the coming decades, such as the home health care industry that provides vital assistance to a growing population of elderly persons.

The expulsion of every single undocumented worker now living in the United States would bring its own set of problems at least as large in scope as the problems generated by their presence here: Entire industries would be left without workers. Other industries would have to raise their wages to attract citizen workers to such a degree that it would be harder to compete with other countries where the cost of labor is lower. In addition, prices of products would have to rise to cover the higher cost of labor, which would have a serious impact on the average consumer's pocketbook.

The inefficiency of the immigration system now in place actually creates the problem of illegality: For decades, not enough visas have been offered for the low-skilled workers that the American economy needs to fill jobs that do not interest an increasingly educated citizenry.

In 1960, half of all Americans in the workforce—particularly men—were high school dropouts who were qualified only for low-skilled jobs in fields like agriculture or construction. Today, fewer than 10 percent of those born in the United States have less than a high school diploma.[1] And although the economy continues to shift toward service and away from manufacturing, the agricultural sector continues to be an important source of jobs.

Basically, over the past several decades, the US economy has generated a significant number of jobs at the lowest skill levels of the workforce ladder, but there are not enough citizens willing or able to take them. The agriculture industry is chronically short of workers, and even in the middle of a recession, it is still shorthanded.

Audrey Singer, a demographer and expert in international migration at the Brookings Institute, points out: "The United States has become a much more educated society than ever before. The number of citizens without a high school diploma continues to decrease, but there is still a persistent demand for labor in fields such as construction or landscaping, jobs that cannot be exported or outsourced to another country, and must be continually filled."[2]

In other words, the US economy has for decades demonstrated an insatiable appetite for immigrant labor, especially at the lowest skill levels, and yet has not provided adequate avenues of legal immigration for these workers. The result of this asymmetry between demand for labor and the legal means of satisfying that demand has been the disproportionate growth in illegal immigration.

Even as the United States struggles through a recession with high levels of unemployment, there are still sectors of the economy that depend on the labor provided by undocumented immigrants. And, as has happened in the past, demand for labor will again increase in some expected areas of the economy and will surge in new sectors.

There are two sides to every story. Although undocumented workers are productive and make a valuable contribution to the economy, their presence does come at a price. Of course, analyzing and defining that price is hardly a simple exercise. Local governments and municipalities are the hardest hit by illegal immigration, since their children, whether themselves US citizens or not, receive a free public education and emergency health care, while undocumented immigrants pay a relatively small amount in property and sales taxes because of their generally low income levels.

Those same immigrants do pay a significant amount in federal social security taxes, especially since the mid-1980s, when the Amnesty Law passed by Reagan required that job seekers present documents proving their eligibility to work. This in turn led to a burgeoning cottage industry producing false documents and selling social security numbers to immigrants. Since then, the Social Security Administration has received a constant stream of contributions from illegal immigrants who have social security tax deducted each week from their paychecks. But, because of their undocumented status they can never collect those benefits themselves. In fact, undocumented immigrants contribute $9 billion in social security taxes every year, of which they will never see a penny.[3]

In other words, the illegal status of these immigrants simultaneously results in a gain and a loss for the US economy. Their lack of legal status depresses wages and means they can be exploited by employers virtually without consequence; but this same cheap labor pool that keeps prices of the goods and services they produce low also has the effect of dragging down the wages of citizens and legal residents performing similar jobs.

Many academic researchers have studied the effect of undocumented workers on the labor force, especially how they affect other immigrants. Economists studying international migration have looked at the issue from every possible angle, and the broadest conclusion that can be drawn has been this: Low-skilled undocumented immigrant workers have had a modest or negligible effect on the wages of similarly skilled workers.[4]

But wages are not the only element of this story: Some researchers conclude that undocumented immigrant labor keeps food prices low; others point out that the overall productivity of undocumented workers ultimately leads to further job creation.[5]

Internet chat rooms, talk radio, and the political debates are full of comments from US citizens railing against "illegals" and the serious damage they are allegedly doing to the ordinary workers in this country. But one can't help but consider the corporate point of view, which must see this vast labor pool who are afraid of being discovered, as a means of paying rock-bottom wages to their workers.

There is another important fact to consider: At least 1 million undocumented immigrants—and this figure is from 2007; the number is probably much higher now—are not employed by major corporations but by individuals, who hire them to work as nannies, housekeepers, and gardeners, and by small business owners, who hire them to staff their restaurants, nail salons, and construction companies, where low labor costs can mean the difference between success and failure.

From this perspective, it's worth considering whether restaurants, shops, and other small businesses could survive without the low-cost labor that immigrants provide. Would there be enough US citizen workers ready to step in and meet the demand for dishwashers, babysitters, housekeepers, and gardeners? Could the US middle and upper-middle classes continue to enjoy the same standard of living they have grown accustomed to over the past few decades without this pool of immigrant workers who are affordable and available unconditionally to perform the most intimate and most difficult jobs around the home? As we can see, the problem is a multifaceted one, with no easy answers.

The key to coming up with meaningful solutions would be finding the middle ground and negotiating a rational immigration policy that would be good for the American economy and the immigrants themselves. The problem is that since the mid-1990s, it has been impossible to have a reasonable discussion on the issue. Politicians have not been able to face the actual needs of the country to construct an immigration policy that works.

Unsurprisingly, the co-opting of the subject of immigration as nothing more than a political tool to manipulate voters and win elections has hardly facilitated sound decision making. Rather, it has given rise to the dysfunctional system that is now in place, which actually harms the country rather than serving its best interests.

For the past twenty years, a neo-nativist mood has prevailed in the United States, so law enforcement measures have been the only politically acceptable means of solving the immigration problem. Virtually nothing has been done to adapt the immigration system to the country's current needs or to maximize how immigrants can benefit the nation through legislation that makes sense for the economy as a whole.

On the contrary, the increasingly restrictive measures have proven to be costly not only for taxpayers but for millions of undocumented immigrants who have been forced into the shadowy underworld of exploitation. Their status—illegal, and devoid of any rights—depresses wages and limits their potential long-term contributions into the US treasury as taxpayers themselves since they are excluded from legal employment.

And if that weren't enough, the illegal status of this vast swath of the population is what seriously impedes meaningful discussion of possible solutions. For many Americans, the debate on the issue begins and ends with the legal status of these immigrants: "What part of 'illegal' don't you understand?" they repeat, deeply disturbed by the presence of undocumented foreigners in their country. "I'm not against immigrants, I'm against *illegal* immigrants," proclaimed the prophet of state-imposed restrictions against immigrants Pete Wilson, California's governor from 1991 until 1998.[6] Many Americans repeat this catchphrase today, and although most accept the presence of legal immigrants, they view illegal immigrants as intolerable.

This attitude is understandable from a sociological perspective. But the illegal status of immigrants stems from political rulings and real economic situations; it is not due to their simple refusal to immigrate legally.

For decades, very little vigilance was exercised along the US borders. To many immigrants, especially those coming from south of the border, crossing it was the only way to enter the mythical promised land of the North and get a job. For the better part of our nation's history, the US economy welcomed and exploited labor provided by immigrants, both legal and undocumented. The country also went through some challenging social changes resulting from new populations of foreigners.

But immigration is an emotional, personal subject, with racially charged connotations. It is a highly volatile, complex issue, which brings few rewards to any politicians who decide to address it as comprehensively and honestly as it merits. Still, the time is fast approaching when the country will not have any choice except to deal with it head-on. Without a detailed analysis of immigration politics, an overhaul of immigration legislation, and a sincere study of the areas of the economy that require workers, whether they are specialized or not, the cost of doing nothing will prove to be unacceptably high for American society and its future.

The vast majority of demographic, sociological, and economic studies conducted by nonpartisan, independent research institutions conclude that the future of this country depends in large part on how immigration is handled and that facilitating an influx of immigrants to meet the country's needs will be indispensable for the United States to maintain its productivity and economic competitiveness over the long term.[7]

This reality applies not only to undocumented immigrants but also to legal ones, a group that, as mentioned, most Americans find much more acceptable. But the fact that immigration programs have not been evaluated and revised in over twenty years adversely affects legal immigrants as well, as the outdated system in place is not up to meeting the challenge of managing future influxes of new immigrants.

In an article titled "America Risks Losing Its Immigration Advantage," journalist Fareed Zakaria asserts that what has kept the United States economically vibrant decade after decade is its diversity and the constant replenishment of its workforce, all thanks to immigration: "Business people will tell you that one of the reasons they still look at the U.S. as a very attractive market for the future is it will have lots of young workers, producers, consumers, investors and spenders. We have this huge strength in immigration. But are we managing it well? Here, once again (alas), you have a case where American society is very dynamic and American politics is completely paralyzed."[8]

Even as the United States remains in the grip of a recession during the second decade of the twenty-first century, there are sound reasons to support the full integration of the immigrants already here and to create a system that would welcome newcomers in order to take advantage of their energy, youth, and high productivity. There are also clear indications of what we can expect if immigration is not dealt with constructively and if we continue to view immigration as a problem, a net negative, and a burden for the great country that is the United States.

To Dowell Myers, the USC demographer and urban planning professor that attitude "is looking backward instead of into the future.

"There is an urgent need for immigration reform. Unfortunately, debates about immigration in America have been backward-looking, emphasizing trends of the last ten years, not the future. In the decade ahead, much will change—immigrants and the rest of us included," Myers explains. "The preoccupation with matters of legal status, important as they are, have distracted us from the larger question of whether we need immigrants in the first place. For that answer we must look more closely at American society itself."[9]

The United States faces the same irrefutable reality as other developed countries face around the world: an aging population, which means rapid growth of the least productive segment of society who have retired after a lifetime of work and are now collecting social security pensions and relying on Medicare, and who in many cases are not financially independent.

For the first time in our history, the United States faces a crisis of aging demographics. The baby boomer generation—the 78 million people born in the post–World War II era of 1946 to 1964—have just begun to be eligible for social security and Medicare, the government insurance program for senior citizens. In the coming years, this generation will retire from the workforce and try to sell their homes. As they age will require medical care, benefits, and an array of social services.

Myers has conducted in-depth research projecting the future needs of the country. It comes down to numbers: the ratio of adults in their most productive years to adults who have retired. Since 1980, this proportion has remained at sustainable levels:

240 retirees for every 1,000 productive adults. But over the coming decades, this ratio will shift dramatically: The number of retirees will rise by 67 percent, so there will be 411 retirees for every 1,000 productive adults. In some states, the ratio will be even higher.[10]

Studies and economic projections have reached similar conclusions for years. The US Bureau of Labor Statistics projects that the labor force will grow at a rate of less than 1 percent per year.[11] Even factoring in delays in retirement caused by the recession, if we maintain the status quo, it will be very difficult to produce enough workers to replace retiring baby boomers. The economy as a whole will certainly suffer.

Myers affirms that immigrants have a great deal to contribute within this context, especially since as a group they are young and have the highest fertility rates. At the present time, the United States still has the immigrant advantage. Even though the number of newcomers arriving, particularly undocumented immigrants, has gone down with the recession, the preceding years of economic prosperity attracted millions of young people in their most productive years at all skill levels.

But the proliferation of punitive laws, the politics of deportation, and an overall lack of interest in educating and integrating immigrants threatens to reverse the contributions of a large group that could significantly alleviate the economic pressures that a country with a rapidly aging population faces.

SIXTEEN
IS THE AMERICAN DREAM DEAD?

Not like the brazen giant of Greek fame
With conquering limbs astride from land to land;
Here at our sea-washed, sunset gates shall stand
A mighty woman with a torch, whose flame
Is the imprisoned lightning, and her name
Mother of Exiles. From her beacon-hand
Glows world-wide welcome; her mild eyes command
The air-bridged harbor that twin cities frame,
"Keep, ancient lands, your storied pomp!" cries she
With silent lips. "Give me your tired, your poor,
Your huddled masses yearning to breathe free,
The wretched refuse of your teeming shore,
Send these, the homeless, tempest-tossed to me,
I lift my lamp beside the golden door!"

—Emma Lazarus, New York City, 1883,
poem inscribed on the Statue of Liberty

We hold these truths to be self-evident, that all men are created
equal, that they are endowed by their Creator with certain inalien-
able rights, that among these are life, liberty and the pursuit of
happiness.

—Preamble of the Declaration of Independence

JUST LIKE THE GENERATIONS OF IMMIGRANTS WHO CAME BEFORE THEM, PRES-
ent-day immigrants come here in search of more than basic
economic subsistence. They carry more than just clothes and
keepsakes from the old country with them in their suitcases; they
also bring along their own version of the myth that has doggedly
persisted after all these years: the American Dream.

The concept of the American Dream is implicit in the most
essential documents of the country's founding and is inscribed at
the base of its most famous symbol: the Statue of Liberty. The preamble of the Declaration of Independence includes a phrase that
is radical even today, and was much more so when it was written
in the eighteenth century, declaring the equality of all men and
their right to "life, liberty and the pursuit of happiness."

The new nation began full of hope while at the same time it
was wracked by the sharp dissonance between its lofty fundamental ideals and reality, a tension that endures to this day.

When George Washington, Thomas Jefferson, James Madison, and the other founding fathers set down on paper the principles that would govern the new country, just as today, all men
were clearly not equal. Women could not vote. Most black men
and women were slaves owned by other people, with no rights
at all.

Even so, over the course of its long history, this country has
been the land of opportunity for millions of immigrants. First
among them were the Europeans who escaped the restrictions of
the Old World in search of the wide open expanses and bound-
less opportunities of the new. Crossing the ocean was a treacherous journey, in squalid conditions that sometimes killed the most
vulnerable passengers, who were buried at sea; likewise, far too

many of their modern-day counterparts succumb to the deadly Arizona desert and mountains, their bones bleached by the sun.

Most of the immigrants of centuries past were poor peasants, just as many are now, and arrived by boat. Often they were conscripted by the shipping companies transporting them to the New World. After several weeks at sea, they finally sailed into New York Harbor, where the magnificent Lady Liberty awaited them. This powerful symbol of what the United States represented was a gift from France and was dedicated in 1886.

The 151-foot-tall statue retains such symbolic power that even visitors today gazing on her get teary-eyed. We can only imagine how overcome with joy earlier immigrants must have felt as they caught their first glimpse of her from their crowded boats, where the poor, tired, huddled masses from teeming shores had spent weeks waiting to start their life anew.

The ideal persists, along with the real-world contradictions.

It is hard to believe that even in today's political environment, the poem by Emma Lazarus inscribed at the base of the Statue of Liberty is still seen as expressing a fundamental principle of our nation. "Give me your tired, your poor,/Your huddled masses yearning to breathe free,/The wretched refuse of your teeming shore,/Send these, the homeless, tempest-tossed to me,/I lift my lamp beside the golden door!"

No matter what their legal status, immigrants from around the world still see the proverbial golden door. However, the political discourse and immigration laws passed over the last twenty years suggest that the United States is mired in one of the most virulently nativist phases this country has ever experienced.

Where did this new sense of doom about immigration come from?

For decades, Gallup, one of the most respected polling organizations in the world, has conducted public opinion polls to determine whether the US public's view of immigrants has changed.

Surprisingly, with very little variation, most Americans continue to believe that immigration is good for the country.

In fact, in polls conducted in 2006, 2008, even in July 2011, in the middle of a serious economic recession, 59 percent of respondents said that immigration is positive for the country, and 64 percent believed that the government should grant legal status to undocumented immigrants who fulfilled certain requirements. At the same time, 53 percent felt that it was "extremely important" to stop illegal immigration.[1]

Overall, the far greater part of the political discussion on immigration focuses on this last point, "illegal"—undocumented or unauthorized immigration. A number of politicians have reinforced the fears of certain sectors of the public who believe illegal immigration is corrosive and its perpetrators among the nation's very worst criminals.

The careful distinction drawn between legal and illegal immigration is the new twist on an ongoing political discourse that was essentially identical before "illegal immigrants" even existed: Some immigrants are good, some are bad. Generally, the "good" ones are the people already here, who came before now (whenever "now" is); and the "bad" are the people just arriving now or who will in the future.

In recent years, the whole concept of illegality has become the biggest stumbling block to a rational dialogue on immigration. "Illegal" is for many a synonym for criminal, and the discussion ends right there: They cannot discuss objectively individual immigrants' merits and the positive role they could play in society and the economy. Instead, the immigrants are cast in a negative light from the outset and seen as a threat.

"[W]e want to build a border fence, instead of analyzing what we have done, economically and demographically, to create a market that attracts them," according to Robert Suro, a journalism professor at the University of Southern California and Marcelo Suarez Orozco, an anthropologist at New York University.[2]

The political discourse that has prevailed since the mid-1990s is largely to blame for emphasizing the threat illegal immigrants pose rather than their positive attributes and the benefits they bring to the country. As a result of politicians' mad rush to pander to the lowest common denominator and placate voters' basest fears of the "other" among us, immigration politics have become counterproductive not only for the immigrants but for the national interest.

Over the past fifteen years, the idealistic nation the Statue of Liberty so powerfully symbolizes has devolved into one that exploits, vilifies, threatens, and routinely violates the human rights of many immigrants, people whose only mistake was coming to this country in search of a better life at a time when the borders are more closely controlled than ever before.

In my work as a journalist reporting on immigration issues in Los Angeles, over the past several years I have written about how the lives of undocumented immigrants have become even more challenging. If achieving the American Dream means enduring the hardships inherent in transitioning to a new country, working tirelessly, and making sacrifices to ensure one's children have a shot at a better life, the current generation of undocumented immigrants—11 million people who came here because there was a job waiting for them, or in the case of children, brought by their families through no fault of their own—are paying a very high price.

In the pages of the newspaper I write for, *La Opinión*, and in many other media outlets across the country, we journalists are not only reporting on the new laws and the political discussion centering around illegal immigrants. We are also covering the cases—dozens, hundreds, maybe thousands and thousands—of undocumented immigrants who instead of finding a better life find themselves trapped in a waking nightmare.

On an episode of the PBS newsmagazine *Frontline*, María Hinojosa reported on conditions in detention centers for immigrants being processed for deportation, in prisons run by Immigration and Customs Enforcement (ICE), and in the many privately run prisons that are reaping the benefits of a flourishing industry that enforces the mandatory incarceration for immigrants in deportation proceedings.[3] One woman who spoke on the condition of anonymity told Hinojosa about her horrifying experience at a detention center in Willacy, Texas, where she was sexually abused for months by a prison guard.

Hinojosa also talked about how thousands of these detainees, most of whom are not felons, have no access to legal counsel. Unlike inmates in the rest of the criminal justice system, undocumented immigrants have no right to an attorney.

Spanish-language media, and to a lesser extent English-language media, have reported on other cases of civil rights violations, such as mentally ill detainees languishing in immigration prisons for years, lost in the system, and the systemic abuse of homosexual and transsexual detainees. The shocking case of Victoria Arellano brought the situation to light. A twenty-three-year-old transgender woman and an AIDS patient, Arellano was denied necessary medications and medical attention, despite the loud protests of her fellow inmates at the detention facility in San Pedro, California. Arellano was finally taken to a hospital, where, on July 20, 2007, she died shackled to a bed, two immigration agents standing guard. She was an unauthorized immigrant but was not accused with any other crime.[4]

Sadly, hard-line immigration policies have had the most devastating impact on families. In one segment on the *Frontline* broadcast, Hinojosa interviewed two children of Antonio and Rosana Arceo, after Rosana was pulled over for speeding and summarily deported without a hearing. There was no time for her family to react; there was no time to even say good-bye.

Her husband, Antonio, has stayed in Maple Park, Illinois. He still working as a mechanic and doing the best he can to raise their children on his own, with the help of their church and friends. The couple's four children are all American citizens.

"What do you think when your dad says maybe you should go back to Mexico?" Hinojosa asks one of the boys, who looks to be around thirteen or fourteen years old.

"I don't know, the thought of having to pack up all my things and leaving my country to go to a country I've never been to doesn't seem right," David answers.

He and his brother said they had dreamed of continuing their studies and having successful careers in their chosen professions. One boy had wanted to be a policeman, but after the immigration officer took his mother away, he's changed his mind. "I don't want to anymore," the boy says.

David had wanted to be a lawyer, a goal that had seemed possible at one time. "I'm more concerned with other things right now," David admits, with the solemnity of someone who has suffered tragedy at a young age.

David has not lost only his mother; he has lost faith in the authority of his country, which treats him and his family as if they do not belong. He also may have lost hope for a better future. For this family, the American Dream disappeared when Rosana was deported.

The story of David and his siblings is hardly unique. At least 5.5 million children in the United States have at least one undocumented parent. The majority of those children—75 percent—are themselves American citizens.

Are we willing to knowingly destroy the lives and families of all of these citizen children? Does this country still need to be convinced that the best overall approach to the problem of the illegal immigrant families in our midst is the integration and education of this young generation, so they can be fully contributing members of society? This need is greater now than ever before in history; these young people can make the difference between a future with an aging population and a nation in decline, or one where the United States maintains its global preeminence, thanks to the youth and diversity of its population.

In 2011 alone, over 400,000 foreigners were deported. Among those, approximately half had committed no crime whatsoever aside from simply being undocumented, which according to US law is a civil, not a criminal, offense. Many others were detained for minor infractions, such as a traffic violation or driving without a license. Programs such as Secure Communities led to their identification and deportation.

Despite their lack of papers, life goes on for millions of immigrants, although it is more difficult than before. For example, twenty years ago it was fairly easy for undocumented immigrants to get driver's licenses; today, hardly any states will grant them licenses.

The lack of access to official, government-granted personal identification has compelled increasing numbers of immigrants to resort to the black market to obtain documentation that will allow them to get a license, a job, and a place to live.

Thanks to federal programs like Secure Communities and Section 287g, which empowers local police officers to act as immigration enforcers, undocumented immigrants find any contact with authorities increasingly problematic, even if they wish to report a crime—since they will very likely be handed over to ICE agents as a result.

Today, a minor traffic violation or even a phone call to the police to report an incident of domestic violence can thrust someone who is undocumented into deportation proceedings. It has happened many times and is often reported in Spanish-language media outlets in particular. For the undocumented community, the United States, the land of freedom and democracy, has become a police state. Living off the radar is essential; having no contact with the police is even more critical.

According to law enforcement officials themselves, this state of affairs is counterproductive for society as a whole. Even many foreign-born legal residents avoid dealing with the police for fear that it could have negative repercussions when they apply for citizenship or, worse yet, that they will somehow wind up in deportation proceedings.

Many police chiefs are opposed to programs like Secure Communities and the local immigration laws specifically because they endanger public safety rather than strengthening it. The list of police associations and individuals who have come out against radical anti-immigrant measures, such as Arizona's SB 1070 is long: It includes former San Francisco chief of police of George Gascon; Sheriff Clarence Dupnik of Pima County, Arizona; the Arizona Association of Chiefs of Police; Robert Davis, president of the Major Cities Chiefs of Police Association of San Jose, California; Police Chief Richard Myers of Colorado Springs; and many others.

"What's going to happen is you're going to fear the police. . . . [Immigrants] are going to shy away from us instead of coming forward with information," stated Sergeant Brian Soller, president of the Mesa Lodge Fraternal Order in Mesa, Arizona.

Also, illegality forces immigrants into the black market for labor, where average wages are often lower than the federally mandated minimum wage. Undocumented immigrants depress the pay scales of jobs that are already poorly compensated, since employers take advantage of their illegal status to pay them as little as they possibly can. If one of the main arguments against undocumented immigrants is that they represent unfair competition for American workers, especially for low-skilled jobs, then maintaining their illegal status indefinitely will serve only to exacerbate the problem.

For example, the *Wall Street Journal* published an article by Miriam Jordan, a journalist who writes on immigration issues, chronicling how life had changed for one immigrant couple who had lived in the United States for more than ten years.[5] Alba and Eugenio lost their jobs working for an office cleaning company, where for over a decade they had earned double the minimum wage, plus benefits. They were fired after the federal government initiated an audit of the company's employee records and they had to take jobs at a smaller company, for half the pay. But the new company was audited too, leaving them unemployed. Now they take whatever odd jobs they can and visit the local food bank when they can't afford to buy groceries. Their story shows how a family that was once comfortably working class can quickly plummet down the economic ladder to join the growing ranks of the poor.

This change in circumstances for newer immigrants will also negatively impact the US economy, because immigrant workers will pay less in taxes, consume less, and contribute less to social security and Medicare.

Adopting hard-line policies against undocumented immigrants is not the magic bullet that many politicians would have you believe. "When I am president, I will put an end to illegal immigration," vows Mitt Romney, Republican candidate for President in 2012. If Romney has the secret formula to actually achieve this, he should have shared it in 2008, during his first campaign for the Republican nomination, or even earlier, during his tenure as governor of Massachusetts.

In fact, when Romney was governor, he did lay out a plan in which he favored a process of legalization for undocumented immigrants, as long as they "got in the back of the line": "[T]he central issue is that people who are here illegally should be able, should not be prohibited, should be able to apply for permanent residency, citizenship, that should not be prohibited, but that they should not receive any special advantage in being granted those, ah . . . status, relative to people that applied legally," Romney said in a 2007 interview with a Florida newspaper.[6]

At the same time, during Barack Obama's presidency, more than 1.2 million undocumented immigrants have been deported.

"We are applying the laws of this country," affirms Cecilia Muñoz, the White House director of Intergovernmental Affairs. Muñoz had been a well-respected organizer for immigrant rights, and her appointment to the White House position was hailed as an achievement by Latino groups. "At the end of the day, when you have immigration law that's broken and you have a community of 10 million, 11 million people living and working in the United States illegally, some of these things are going to happen. Even if the law is executed with perfection, there will be parents separated from their children. They don't have to like it, but it is a result of having a broken system of laws."[7]

The positions of the Democratic Party, supposedly the more progressive political party, sometimes seem just as dubious on immigration as those of their Republican counterparts. Muñoz, who had been one of the most prominent pro-immigrant activists in Washington for years and had risen to the level of vice president of the National Council of La Raza, knows perfectly well that deportation policies are not going to put a stop to illegal immigration. The only way to stop immigration is to eliminate the jobs that the undocumented workers come here to fill.

Why do the prevailing dialogue and hard-line policies continue, when public opinion is actually much more rational than what is reflected in the news?

They persist because everything in politics is local. The first shot was fired across the bow in California in 1994, to rescue the flagging reelection prospects of a Republican governor. In

Hazleton, Pennsylvania, in 2006, a mayor manipulated and exploited the fear of change and bias of the local populace in the face of a steep influx of immigrants in order to get himself elected to Congress.

In 2011, the Republican candidates for the presidential nomination engaged in fierce competition—not to see who could best pull the country out of a stubborn recession but to demonstrate who could take the hardest line against undocumented immigrants. The conservative base of their party was the target audience for their message and the group they needed to please the most.

Like Bill Clinton before him, Barack Obama never wanted to be viewed as favoring illegal immigrants by aggressively pushing immigration reform or by slowing down the breakneck pace of deportations. As the 2012 elections drew nearer, he had to make some difficult decisions and come up with some solutions to the problems his aggressive immigration policies were creating, in particular with Latino voters.

Latino voters and naturalized citizens from other countries do not yet possess the electoral power to uniformly sway the positions that candidates and politicians take on immigration. In most areas of the country, the average voter is still white and middle-aged or older, a group that tends to vote more conservatively in general on this issue.

In sum, the undocumented immigrant is one of the most useful and most highly politicized entities in the United States today. Here I would like to borrow the views of a mentor and good friend, the journalist Rafael Buitrago, who summarized what the undocumented immigrant means to this country.

"They are the most productive of all, since everyone benefits from their presence here in one way or another. They pick our fruits and vegetables, mow our lawns, care for our children and seniors, clean our houses, and cook our meals. They work hard, for long hours and are consumers, and pay taxes, and contribute to the economies of their countries of origin. And on top of all that, they help politicians to win elections," Rafael told me as we talked about the issues in this chapter.

At other times in this country's history, the waves of anti-immigrant sentiment have ebbed—without ever disappearing altogether—once the economy improved. So as long as the current recession hangs on, the demonizing of immigrants will continue unabated.

The federal government needs to take a good hard look at the immigration system in place. If we are so opposed to illegal immigration, why not change the laws in order to create legal avenues of immigration that would suit the needs of the labor market and the economy? How strongly do conservatives, the group most in favor of restrictive anti-immigrant measures, actually believe in a real free market, which should include the unrestricted flow of legalized labor, as the market itself demands?

If we don't want to legalize 11 million undocumented immigrants, deporting them all is not a realistic solution either. At a cost of $23,000 per deportation, even if it were achievable, the tab would be $253 billion, billed to US taxpayers. How can this impasse in reforming the legal immigration system of this country be overcome?

Maintaining a population of 11 million people in a state of permanent illegality does not benefit anyone. There has never been a time when so many immigrants to America have been forced to exist in a state of illegality for so long, with the notable exception of the Chinese, who were barred from attaining citizenship for over sixty years. This protracted life in the shadows has consequences: limited participation in society as a whole and in the economy, rampant exploitation in the workplace, and generally a much more difficult time integrating into the new country.

Nevertheless, the American Dream remained intact through even harder times: the Civil War, the Great Depression, both world wars, and numerous other economic crises. Its attraction burns ever bright, like Lady Liberty's torch. Each generation of newcomers may harbor some doubts, but young men and women continue to pack their suitcases full of dreams and set off for the land where they believe a more promising future awaits.

SEVENTEEN
DEMOGRAPHIC CHANGE
WON'T WAIT

THE AMERICAN DREAM IS ALIVE AND WELL AMONG THE LATEST GENERATION OF immigrants and their children; just attend any one of the many naturalization ceremonies that take place around the country every month to see it in action.

In October 2011, two naturalization ceremonies were held in the Los Angeles Convention Center on the same day, one in the morning and one in the afternoon. In all, twelve thousand new American citizens took an oath of allegiance to their new country that day in Los Angeles alone.

Every ceremony is highly emotional. Even for those who are not usually given to patriotic sentimentality, the naturalization ceremony is full of powerful symbolism, stirring up emotions not easily controlled. I still remember very clearly what I felt on May 25, 2000, when along with five or six thousand others I took the oath of allegiance and received my certificate of US citizenship.

I remember the cavernous room bursting with collective emotion, full of waving flags and a sea of faces, some smiling, others solemn. Some cried, some laughed, but no one was indifferent. Speeches were given, inspiring the newest American citizens to remain steadfast in their commitment to their adopted homeland.

We felt grateful for our new country's generosity, even though the long journey to that ceremony had been far from easy.

Every year, the United States grants 1 million immigrants legal residency and allows approximately another million legal residents to become naturalized citizens. Despite the new restrictions, the United States continues to welcome more legal immigrants than any other country in the world and it also continues to benefit greatly from them.

In the words of Joel Kotkin, writer and professor of urban development at Chapman University in Orange, California, and author of *The Next Hundred Million: America in 2050,* "Immigration is a vote for America."[1]

"People come here, they're choosing to come here, they overcome tremendous obstacles to come here and they replenish our society and we've done a reasonably good job at integrating them," asserts Kotkin.

Instead of raising red flags about the possible threat illegal immigration poses, or the dangers of a growing population, Kotkin lays out a hopeful vision of America.[2] He believes that we have the potential to maintain our place as a global leader not in spite of, but because of, our abundant immigrant population:

"The U.S. has got a very different demographic trajectory than other countries we compare ourselves with, most particularly some in East Asia and Europe, that means we have a different set of opportunities and challenges. I'm basically optimistic because I think it's much better to have a younger growing population than an older shrinking population."[3]

Immigrants and their children revitalize cities that have been in decline for decades, Kotkin points out. "There were many cities around the country that were rapidly losing residents, which are now home to new immigrants, and being revitalized in every way. . . . America will be a very diverse country, but it will be diverse in its diversity. I don't believe we'll have these very un-melted groups of Hispanics that only speak Spanish, or Chinese or any other group that isolates—it will be a lot of blending, there will be tremendous growth in the mixed race population, and an American culture that will be very different from what it is now." Kotkin talks about an optimistic United States with the same American Dream at its heart that has been there since the nation's founding, but comprised of a more diverse mix of ethnic and cultural groups, increasingly open and tolerant socially and culturally and highly aware of our responsibility to protect the environment.

Right now, that dream seems threatened by a protracted economic recession and by a widening gap between the rich and the poor that is chipping away at what has always made this country work: a solid, strong middle class. From different points of view, the Tea Party and the Occupy movement—a global protest movement against economic inequality that first took hold in the United States in September 2011—are both reactions from an American middle class that under siege and increasingly aware that the current legal immigration system needs to undergo fundamental change before it can meet the needs of present-day America.

In the meantime, population shifts do not wait or ask for permission before taking effect. The 2011 census profiled a racially and ethnically diverse nation, with a non-Hispanic white population of 64 percent, the lowest percentage in history, and a Hispanic population making up 16 percent of the total, the largest minority racial group in the country at this point (African Americans were counted at 12.6 percent of the country's total population in 2012). By the middle of the twenty-first century, whites will no longer comprise an absolute majority of the US population. As a percentage of the total, the numbers of whites will decline, making room for minority groups of diverse races and growing numbers of people of mixed races and ethnicities.

Interracial marriages have reached record numbers, and this trend will only grow in future generations, as ethnic and racial blending become the rule, not the exception.

The largest segment of the immigrant population in recent years—Latinos—is now the fasting-growing segment of the population overall. Most of that growth is now attributed to the numbers of Latinos born in the United States, not to immigration. The 2011 census counted 50 million Latinos in the country.

Polls have repeatedly shown that Latinos, whether they immigrated to this country or were born here, have an open, tolerant views on immigration.

If there is one group that is unhappy with the wave of anti-immigrant legislation at the local and state level and the political standstill at the federal level that has made the introduction and passage of meaningful reform impossible, it is Latinos living here.

Shifting demographics and the integration of new Latino voters into US politics will result in an overall change in attitude toward immigrants in the near future, for one simple reason: Latino voters are extremely close to the immigrant experience themselves, just as immigrants from other backgrounds were at their moment in history.

A poll of Latino voters conducted by Impremedia and Latino Decisiones in 2011 found that 53 percent of Latino voters know someone who is undocumented and 25 percent know a person or family that has been deported or is currently in deportation proceedings.[4] This personal proximity translates into extremely high levels of support—between 70 and 80 percent—for legalization and integration of undocumented immigrants into society.

Alarmed by the rising waves of nativism and hostility directed at their immigrant brothers and sisters, Latino voters have an emphatically pro-immigrant political stance. They expect their representatives to treat honest, hard-working immigrants who are here in search of a better life fairly and respectfully.

This segment of the American population knows that a vote in favor of the "good" immigrant who comes here to make an honest living is also a vote for the future of this country, which has been the biggest test lab for immigration in the entire world.

If the United States still has a future as a world power, it is thanks to, not in spite of, its immigrants—those of today and those who came before. But that will continue to be true only if our leaders possess the necessary vision to see that the fact of immigration is in itself a huge vote for America.

The time has come for the current generation of US leaders to cast a vote for its immigrants as well.

NOTES

FOREWORD

1. With some exceptions: Barbara Lee, a congresswoman from California, refuses to use self-service checkout lanes in supermarkets on the grounds that they put cashiers out of work.
2. Stephen Moore and Julian Simon, *It's Getting Better All the Time: 100 Greatest Trends of the Last 100 Years* (Washington, DC: Cato Institute, 2000), 52.
3. "Not Coming to America: Why the US is Falling Behind in the Global Race for Talent," report by The Partnership for a New American Economy and the Partnership for New York City, May 2012, http://www.renewour economy.org/sites/all/themes/pnae/not-coming-to-america.pdf, 6–8.
4. Madeline Zavodny, "Immigration and American Jobs," American Enterprise Institute and Partnership for a New American Economy, December 2011, http://www.aei.org/paper/society-and-culture/immigration /immigration-and-american-jobs/.
5. Stuart Anderson, "Immigrant Founders and Key Personnel in America's 50 Top Venture-Funded Companies," National Foundation for American Policy, NFAP Policy Brief, December 2011, http://www.nfap.com/pdf/NFAP PolicyBriefImmigrantFoundersandKeyPersonnelinAmericasTopVenture FundedCompanies.pdf.
6. For more on this subject, see Robert Guest, *Borderless Economics: Chinese Sea Turtles, Indian Fridges and the New Fruits of Global Capitalism* (New York: Palgrave Macmillan, 2011).

INTRODUCTION

1. Dowell Myers, professor at the University of Southern California School of Policy, Planning, and Development, interview with the author, n.d.
2. On June 15, 2012, President Barack Obama announced that his administration would stop deporting young undocumented immigrants who met certain conditions, granting them deferred action on a case-by-case basis. The estimates of how many "dreamers" would benefit vary from 800,000 to 1.4 million.
3. On June 25, 2012, the Supreme Court of the United States struck down key provisions of Arizona's SB1070 law except Section 2B, which requires a police officer to check immigration status of a suspect, but warned of further legal action if applied too broadly. Soon after, the states of Alabama

and Georgia, enjoined for months from applying their similar laws, went back to appeals court to ask for reconsideration.

4. Editorial, "Immigration Hardball," *The New York Times,* November 14, 2010, http://www.nytimes.com/2010/11/15/opinion/15mon1.html.
5. On June 21, 2012, Republican presidential nominee Mitt Romney offered for the first time more detailed plans for fixing legal immigration to the United States. He offered to expand legal immigration for immediate family members of US resident aliens but maintained opposition to legalizing those who were already here. He also opposes legalization of dreamers with the exception of those in military service.

CHAPTER 1   "I BELIEVE IN AMNESTY"

1. "Candidates Reagan & Bush-41 Discuss Illegal Immigration in 1980 Debate," 1980 Republican presidential primary debate, YouTube, http://www.youtube.com/watch?v=Ixi9_cciy8w.
2. "A Reagan Legacy: Amnesty for Illegal Immigrants," NPR, July 4, 2010, http://www.wbur.org/npr/128303672/a-reagan-legacy-amnesty-for-illegal-immigrants.
3. Rubén Navarrette, "Q&A: Alan Simpson; 1986 Immigration Reform Legislation," *San Diego Union Tribune,* May 28, 2006, http://www.utsandiego.com/uniontrib/20060528/news_z1e28simpson.html.
4. "A Reagan Legacy," NPR.
5. "1984—Ronald Reagan on Amnesty," 1984 Presidential debate between Ronald Reagan and Walter Mondale, YouTube, http://www.youtube.com/watch?v=JfHKIq5z80U.
6. Romano L. Mazzoli and Alan K. Simpson, "Enacting Immigration Reform, Again," *Washington Post,* September 15, 2006.
7. Susan H. Welin, "The Effect of Employer Sanctions on Employment Discrimination and Illegal Immigration," *Boston College Third World Law Journal* vol. 9, issue 2 (June 1989): Article 3.

CHAPTER 2   CALIFORNIA CASTS THE FIRST STONE

1. Leonard W. Labaree, ed. *The Papers of Benjamin Franklin,* vol. 4 (New Haven, CT: Yale University Press, 1959), 234.
2. California Legislative Analyst Office, *The California Economy,* January 1995, http://www.lao.ca.gov/1995/010195_calguide/cgep1.html.
3. Gebe Martinez and Doreen Carvajal, "Creators of Prop. 187 Largely Escape Spotlight: Ballot: From secret O.C. location, political novices and veterans spawn strong drive against illegal immigration," *Los Angeles Times,* September 4, 1994, http://articles.latimes.com/1994-09-04/news/mn-34888_1_illegal-immigrants.
4. SCOTUS, Plyler v Doe, No. 80-1538 Argued: December 1, 1981—Decided: June 15, 1982, Cornell University Law School, http://www.law.cornell.edu/supct/html/historics/USSC_CR_0457_0202_ZO.html.
5. Martinez and Carvajal, "Creators of Prop. 187 Largely Escape Spotlight."
6. "Federation for American Immigration Reform," group profile, Southern Poverty Law Center, http://www.splcenter.org/get-informed/intelligence-files/groups/federation-for-american-immigration-reform-fair.

7. Kevin Johnson, *The "Huddled Masses" Myth: Immigration and Civil Rights* (Philadelphia: Temple University Press, 2003), 43.
8. Associated Press, "Immigration Stance Helps Wilson's Rating," *Los Angeles Times,* August 21, 1993, http://articles.latimes.com/1993-08-21/local/me-25984_1_illegal-immigrants.
9. Ronald Brownstein and Patrick J. McDonnell, "Kemp, Bennett and INS Chief Decry Prop. 187: Campaign: Statements by GOP leaders, Clinton Administration official broaden opposition on two fronts," *Los Angeles Times,* October 19, 1994, http://articles.latimes.com/1994-10-19/news/mn-52096_1_illegal-immigrants.
10. Ibid.
11. Ibid.
12. Leslie Berenstein, "Border Death Numbers Remain Steady," *San Diego Union-Tribune,* September 30, 2009, http://www.utsandiego.com/news/2009/sep/30/border-death-numbers-remain-steady/.

CHAPTER 3 NATIVISM

1. From President Grover Cleveland's 1897 Veto Message on House bill 7864, which, among other things, would have excluded the entry of "illiterates" to keep out "undesirables."
2. *Immigration to the United States, 1789–1930,* Harvard University Library Open Collections Program, Digitized Archival Materials, The Immigration Restriction League, http://ocp.hul.harvard.edu/immigration/restrictionleague.html.
3. Mae M. Ngai, *Impossible Subjects: Illegal Aliens and the Making of Modern America* (Princeton, NJ: Princeton University Press, 2005), 30.
4. Mae M. Ngai, professor of history at Columbia University, interview with author, June 30, 2011.
5. Ngai, *Impossible Subjects,* 64.
6. Lamar Smith, "Immigration Reform Is Not Anti-Immigrant," *Las Vegas Sun,* March 6, 1996, http://www.lasvegassun.com/news/1996/mar/06/lamar-smith-immigration-reform-is-not-anti-immigra/.
7. Kevin Johnson, dean of the School of Law at the University of California at Davis, interview with author, October 18, 2011.
8. Sherry Bebitch Jeffe, senior fellow at the School of Policy, Planning and Development at the University of Southern California, interview with the author, October 20, 2011.
9. Doris Meissner, INS commissioner, prepared remarks for press release, "Keeping Our Communities Safe Is INS' Top Priority," April 18, 2000.
10. Doris Meissner, "1996 Immigration Law Overreached," American Immigration Lawyers Association Infonet, March 22, 1996.

CHAPTER 5 IMMIGRATION

1. Mae M. Ngai, *Impossible Subjects: Illegal Aliens and the Making of Modern America* (Princeton, NJ: Princeton University Press, 2005), 37–50.
2. John Ashcroft, *Attorney General Statement Regarding Airport Security Initiative,* Department of Justice news release, April 23, 2002, http://www.justice.gov/opa/pr/2002/April/02_ag_246.htm.

3. US General Accounting Office, "Overstay Tracking: A Key Component of Homeland Security and a Layered Defense," May 2004, Report to the Chairman, Committee on the Judiciary, House of Representatives, pp. 24–27, http://www.gao.gov/new.items/d0482.pdf.

4. Pilar Marrero, "Ataques terroristas desviaron avances del plan migratorio," *La Opinión,* August 28, 2011.

5. Ibid.

6. Maryellen Fullerton, professor at Brooklyn Law School, interviewed by the author, August 2011.

7. Marrero, "Attaques terroristas desviaron avances del plan migratorio."

8. Doris Meissner, director of the US Immigration and Policy Program at the Migratory Policy Institute, interviewed by the author, March 2011.

9. "Immigration Enforcement Since 9/11: A Reality Check," Transactional Records Access Clearinghouse, Syracuse University, September 2011, http://trac.syr.edu/immigration/reports/260/.

10. Sue Long, director, Transactional Records Access Clearinghouse (TRAC), Syracuse University, interview with the author, http://www.impre.com/noticias/2011/12/6/siguen-deportando-a-mas-indocu-285660-1.html.

11. Julie Myers, remarks by Assistant Secretary U.S. Immigration and Customs Enforcement, Department of Homeland Security, American Immigration Lawyers Association Conference, June 14, 2007.

CHAPTER 6   "ILLEGALS" AND THE NEW HATE MOVEMENT

1. Nicolas Ricardi, "Mother Describes Border Vigilante Killings in Arizona," *Los Angeles Times,* January 25, 2011, http://articles.latimes.com/2011/jan/25/news/arizona-test.

2. Pilar Marrero, "Inician juicio a Minuteman por asesinato de niña hispana," *La Opinión,* January 2011.

3. *Jon and Ken Show,* KFI Radio, interview with Governor Arnold Schwarzenegger, April 25, 2005.

4. Peter Baker, "U.S. Mexico and Canada Agree to Increase Cooperation," *Washington Post,* March 24, 2005, http://www.washingtonpost.com/wp-dyn/articles/A59180-2005Mar23.html.

5. Leo R. Chavez, "Spectacle in the Desert: The Minuteman Project on the U.S.-Mexico Border," in David Pratten and Atryee Sen, eds., *Global Vigilantes* (New York: Columbia University Press, 2007), 41.

6. David Kelly, "Border Vigilantes Capture Their Prey, the Media," *Los Angeles Times,* April 5, 2005, http://articles.latimes.com/2005/apr/05/nation/na-minuteman5.

7. Ibid.

8. Minuteman Project website, http://www.minutemanproject.com/.

9. Amy Taxin, "Minutemen Leader Laments Paths of Anti-illegal Immigration Groups," *Orange County Register,* June 25, 2008, http://www.ocregister.com/news/immigration-173479-gilchrist-border.html.

10. Southern Poverty Law Center, "The Second Wave: The Return of the Militias," August 2009, http://www.splcenter.org/sites/default/files/downloads/The_Second_Wave.pdf.

11. ADL news release, "ADL Says Armed Anti-Immigration Groups in Arizona Share Ties to White Supremacists," May 6, 2003, http://www.adl.org/PresRele/Militi_71/4255_72.htm.

12. Associated Press, "Report Says Hate Crimes Increase Against Latinos," Chron.com, March 18, 2008, http://blog.chron.com/immigration/2008/03/report-says-hate-crimes-increase-against-latinos/. ·

13. Pilar Marrero, "Actualidad Política," weekly column, *La Opinión,* May 5, 2009.

14. Pilar Marrero, "¿Y si fuera al revés?" political blog, *La Opinión,* May 2009.

CHAPTER 7   STATES TAKE THE LAW INTO THEIR OWN HANDS

1. US Census, Hazleton, Pennsylvania, http://quickfacts.census.gov/qfd/states/42/4233408.html.

2. US Census, Pahrump, Nevada, http://quickfacts.census.gov/qfd/states/32/3253800.html.

3. Professor Gary Painter, economist at the University of Southern California, interviewed by author, August 2011.

4. Kevin O'Neil, researcher at Princeton University's Demographics Department, interviewed by author, August 2011.

5. Lynette Curtis, "Pahrump Targets Illegal Immigrants," *Las Vegas Review Journal,* November 15, 2006, http://www.reviewjournal.com/lvrj_home/2006/Nov-15-Wed-2006/news/10847735.html.

6. Ibid.

7. Devin Dwyer, "Kansas State Rep. Under Fire for Illegal Immigrant, Feral Hog Comparison," ABC NEWS, March 25, 2011, http://abcnews.go.com/Politics/kansas-rep-fire-comparing-illegal-immigrants-feral-hogs/story?id=13223497.

8. Curtis Cartier, "Loren Nichols, Kennewick City Council Candidate: Kill Illegal Immigrants, Outlaw Spanish," *Seattle Weekly,* August 11, 2011, http://blogs.seattleweekly.com/dailyweekly/2011/08/loren_nichols_ken newick_city_c.php.

CHAPTER 8   HAZLETON, PENNSYLVANIA

1. Michael Powell and Michelle García, "Pa. City Puts Illegal Immigrants on Notice," *Washington Post,* August 22, 2006, http://www.washingtonpost.com/wp-dyn/content/article/2006/08/21/AR2006082101484.html.

2. David Sosar, professor at Kings College, Wilkes-Barre, Pennsylvania, interviewed by author, n.d..

3. "Pennsylvania Attorney General Tom Corbett Talks about Operation Boomerang," video, *Times Leader* (Pennsylvania), September 7, 2007, http://timesleader.magnify.net/video/Corbett-on-Operation-Boomeran.

4. Ibid.

5. Dan Gilgoff, "A Town in Need of a Tomorrow: Letter from Pennsylvania," *US News and World Report,* December 1, 2002, http://www.usnews.com/usnews/news/articles/021209/archive_038355.htm.

6. Powell and García, "Pa. City Puts Illegal Immigrants on Notice."

7. Mark Katchur, "Census: 37% of Hazleton residents ID'd as Hispanic," *Hazleton Standard Speaker,* March 10, 2011.

8. Ibid.

9. "Barletta Speaks on the House Floor," Rep. Lou Barletta channel, YouTube, May 26, 2011, http://www.youtube.com/watch?v=MnW-1zWM8iM&list=UUhViw1Iv0nY1b3Qq9Q0vDBQ&index=4&feature=plcp.

CHAPTER 9   ARIZONA, ALABAMA, AND KOBACH'S ANTI-IMMIGRANT LAWS

1. Valeria Fernández, Phoenix independent journalist, interviewed by author, May 2011.
2. This is referred to as "preemption." The preemption doctrine derives from the Supremacy Clause in the Constitution (Article VI, Clause 2), which says that when there's a conflict, the Constitution and federal law are the supreme law of the land. An example of a state initiative being nullified by this doctrine was the ruling by a federal judge on March 13, 1998 that decided that sections 1 and 4 through 9 of Proposition 187 passed in California in November 1994 to prevent undocumented aliens from receiving health care or education services, are preempted by the federal PRA, IIRAIRA, and other federal law.
3. Quinn Bowman, "Arizona Immigration Law Has Broad Support across US, New Polls Show," PBS News Blog, May 13, 2010.
4. Jessica Vaughan, "Attrition Through Enforcement: A Cost-Effective Strategy to Shrink the Illegal Population," CIS (Center for Immigration Studies) Reports, April 2006, http://www.cis.org/Enforcement-Illegal Population.
5. Southern Poverty Law Center, "WITAN Memo" III by John Tanton, written October 10, 1986, published in the summer of 2002 by the SPLC.
6. Ibid.
7. On June 25, 2012, the Supreme Court of the United States struck down key provisions of Arizona's SB1070 law except Section 2B, which requires a police officer to check immigration status of a suspect but warned of further legal action if applied too broadly.
8. CLU Newsroom, "ACLU And Civil Rights Groups File Legal Challenge To Arizona Racial Profiling Law," May 17, 2010.
9. George Talbott, "Kris Kobach, the Kansas Lawyer Behind Alabama's Immigration Law," Blog Al.Com, October 16, 2011, http://blog.al.com/live/2011/10/kris_kobach_the_kansas_lawyer_1.html.
10. America's Voice en Español website, http://americasvoiceespanol.com.
11. K. Michael Prince, Rally 'Round the Flag Boys (Columbia, SC: University of South Carolina Press), 141.
12. Dan Murtaugh, "Unemployment Rate Falls, but Economist Says Optimism over Figures Should Be Guarded," Alabama Press Register, January 20, 2012.
13. Bob Lowry, "Economists Say Alabama's Tough New Immigration Law Could Damage State's Economy," Huntsville Times (Alabama), July 16, 2011.
14. Phillip Rawls, "Alabama GOP Leaders Have 2nd thoughts on Immigration," Associated Press, December 8, 2011.
15. Ibid.
16. Ibid.
17. Editorial, "Hey Mercedes, Time to Move to a More Welcoming State," St. Louis Post Dispatch, November 22, 2011.

CHAPTER 10   THE BOOMING BUSINESS OF IMMIGRANT DETENTION

1. Laura Sullivan, "Prison Economics Help Drive Ariz. Immigration Law," NPR Report, February 22, 2012, http://www.npr.org/2010/10/28/130833741/prison-economics-help-drive-ariz-immigration-law.

2. Ibid.
3. Ibid.
4. Pico National Network and Public Campaign, "How the Private Prison Industry is Corrupting Our Democracy and Promoting Mass Incarceration," *Unholy Alliance,* November 15, 2011, http://publicampaign.org/reports /unholyalliance.
5. Emily Tucker, investigator for Detention Watch Network, interviewed by author, June 29, 2011.
6. "About The U.S. Detention and Deportation System," http://www.detention watchnetwork.org/aboutdetention.
7. ACLU, "Ten Years Later: Surveillance in the 'Homeland,'" *Truthout* and ACLU, September 2011.
8. *GeoWorld* magazine, June 2011.
9. Charles Ryan, "Biennial Comparison Private vs. Public Provision of Services," December 2010, Arizona Department of Correction.
10. Emily Tucker, interviewed by the author.
11. Center for Responsive Politics, The Revolving Door, http://www.open secrets.org/revolving/.

CHAPTER 11   REJECTING EXTREMISM AND THE SEARCH FOR SOLUTIONS

1. Glenn Barr, "Donnelly Immigration Bills Killed," *Crestline Courier News,* April 2010.
2. Patrick McGreevy and Anthony York, "Brown Signs California Dream Act," *Los Angeles Times,* October 9, 2011, http://articles.latimes.com /2011/oct/09/local/la-me-brown-dream-act-20111009.
3. Ibid.
4. Robert Holguin, "Calif. Dream Act Signed into Law; Donnelly Promises Referendum," KABC Channel 7, Los Angeles, October 10, 2011, http:// abclocal.go.com/kabc/story?section=news/state&id=8386759.
5. "USC College/Los Angeles Times Poll Reveals Shift in Attitudes Regarding Undocumented," April 2010. http://dornsife.usc.edu/usc-lat-poll -undocumented-immigrants-april-2010/.
6. Melissa Sardeli, "Chafee Signs Order to Reverse E-Verify," January 5, 2011, http://www.wpri.com/dpp/news/politics/local_politics/providence -governor-lincoln-chafee-signs-order-to-reverse-e-verify.
7. A bill introduced in May 2012 in the California legislature with bipartisan support, proposes creating a program to issue work and residency permits in the state for undocumented immigrants who meet certain criteria and where there's a need for workers at the time. Democratic assemblyman Felipe Fuentes of Los Angeles is the bill's main sponsor.
8. KSL.com Utah, "Utah Governor Signs Immigration Bills into Law," March 15, 2011, http://www.ksl.com/?nid=960&sid=14740983.

CHAPTER 12   IMMIGRANT YOUTH AND THE BROKEN DREAM

1. Alphonso Chardy, "Miami Student Leader Reveals He Is an Undocumented Migrant," *Miami Herald,* November 2010.
2. "Grecia Lima: Story of Self Us and Now," YouTube, http://www.youtube .com/watch?v=rE8zZ8p13NY; Grecia Lima, "Commencement 2008 Senior Remarks," http://roosevelt.ucsd.edu/student-life/commencement/high lights08/senior-remarks.html.

3. In 2011 California passed two laws, AB130 and AB131, named the California Dream Act. They were signed by the governor, in June and October respectively, and they allow undocumented children who were brought to the United States before the age of 16 and meet certain criteria to apply for student financial aid benefits. The first law addresses private scholarships and the second deals with public scholarships.

4. *Orlando Sentinel,* July 2009.

5. Paul Steinhauser, "Poll: 54 Percent Support DREAM Act," *Political Ticker,* December 10, 2010, http://politicalticker.blogs.cnn.com/2010/12/10/poll -54-percent-support-dream-act/.

6. Immigration Policy Center, "The DREAM Act," http://www.immigration policy.org/just-facts/dream-act.

7. William Gheen, "Dream Act Amnesty Equals The Destruction of America," ALIPAC, December 16, 2010, http://www.alipac.us/f8/dream-act -amnesty-equals-destruction-america-211101/.

8. John Tanton website, http://www.johntanton.org/

9. Federation of Americans for Immigration Reform, "Taxpayers Subsidizing College for Illegal Aliens (2003)," http://www.fairus.org/issue/taxpayers -subsidizing-college-for-illegal-aliens.

10. After President Obama announced his new policy of considering deferred action for Dreamers, CIS published a release saying that it was "Amnesty by Executive Fiat," condemning the action in the usual alarmist terms: "The White House decision to enact the DREAM Act through executive fiat is a lawless act. Any DREAM Act supporter who applauds this measure has forfeited any right to complain about future usurpation of the Constitution."

11. Will Perez, "A New Civil Rights Movement, Undocumented Students for Immigration Reform," *Huffington Post,* February 24, 2010, http://www .huffingtonpost.com/will-perez-phd/a-new-civil-rights-moveme_b_475479 .html.

12. Edgar Santos, interviewed by author, February 2011.

13. Immigration Policy Center, "Dreams Deferred, The Cost of Ignoring Undocumented Students," citing the RAND study, October 18, 2008, http:// www.immigrationpolicy.org/just-facts/dreams-deferred-costs-ignoring -undocumented-students.

14. UCLA North American Integration and Development Center, "No Dreamers Left Behind," December 2010, http://naid.ucla.edu/uploads /4/2/1/9/4219226/no_dreamers_left_behind.pdf.

CHAPTER 13   THE OBAMA ERA

1. Jeffrey Passell, "Size and Characteristics of the Unauthorized Migrant Population in the U.S.," Pew Research Center, March 7, 2006, http://www .pewhispanic.org/2006/03/07/size-and-characteristics-of-the-unauthorized -migrant-population-in-the-us/.

2. "McCain Would Vote Against His Own Immigration Bill," Republican debate, Reagan Library, YouTube, January 30, 2008, http://www.youtube .com/watch?v=AtHOkSWCr6Q.

3. Politifact, The Obameter, "Introduce a Comprehensive Reform Bill First Year," August 13, 2010, http://www.politifact.com/truth-o-meter/promises

/obameter/promise/525/introduce-comprehensive-immigration-bill-first
-yea/.

4. Nick Martin, "'Nothing Changes': How Sheriff Joe Arpaio Went To Battle
Against Civil Rights Lawyers Back in 1997," *TPM Muckraker,* May 11,
2012, http://tpmmuckraker.talkingpointsmemo.com/2012/05/sheriff_joe
_arpaio_civil_rights_1997_battle.php.

5. Tom Zoellner, "Partners in Pink Underwear: Janet Napolitano's Embar-
rassing History with Sherriff Arpaio," *Slate,* November 28, 2008, http://
www.slate.com/articles/news_and_politics/politics/2008/11/partners_in
_pink_underwear.html.

6. Clint Bolick, "Mission Unaccomplished: The Misplaced Priorities of the
Maricopa County Sheriff's Office," Goldwater Institute, December 2, 2008,
http://goldwaterinstitute.org/article/mission-unaccomplished-misplaced
-priorities-maricopa-county-sheriffs-office.

7. Pilar Marrero, "Entrevista con Barack Obama," *La Opinión,* Los Angeles,
May 2008.

8. ICE, news release, "Secretary Napolitano Announces Record-Breaking Immigration Enforcement Statistics Achieved under the Obama Administration," October 2010.

9. Lamar Smith, Committee of the Judiciary, Subcommittee on Immigra
tion Policy and Enforcement Hearing on the E-Verity–Preserving Jobs for
American Workers, February 10, 2011, http://judiciary.house.gov/news
/Statement02102011.html.

10. Immigration Policy Center, "A Framework for Effective Immigration Work-
site Employer Enforcement," January 25, 2011, http://www.immigration
policy.org/just-facts/framework-effective-immigration-worksite-employer
-enforcement.

11. Jeffrey Passel, D'Vera Cohn, "U.S. Unauthorized Immigration Flows Are
Down Sharply Since Mid-Decade," Pew Research Center, September 1,
2010.

12. Leah Muse-Orlinoff, "Staying Put but Still in the Shadows Undocumented
Immigrants Remain in the Country Despite Strict Laws," Center for American Progress, February 2012.

13. Alice Lipowicz, "Witnesses, E-Verify Can't Detect Identity Theft," *Federal
Computer Week,* July 22, 2009.

14. Rubén Navarrette, "Smith Creates Own Reality," *Longview News-Journal,*
May 29, 2011, http://www.news-journal.com/opinion/article_3b9fd4d8
-72cd-539f-9a73-0920e9c57e7c.html.

15. CNN Political Unit, "CNN Poll: Congressional Approval Hits All-Time
Low," January 16, 2012, http://politicalticker.blogs.cnn.com/2012/01/16
/cnn-poll-congressional-approval-hits-all-time-low/.

16. Fran Spielman, "Chicago Aldermen Urge Moratorium on 'Cruel Deportations,'" *Chicago Sun-Times,* January 13, 2011, http://www.suntimes.com
/news/metro/3295280-418/immigration-aldermen-reform-chicago-issue
.html.

17. Maribel Hastings, "Ver para creer," *America's Voice en Español,* August 22, 2011, http://americasvoiceespanol.com/analisis/archive/ver_para
_creer/.

18. On July 10, 2012, ICE director John Morton testified in Congress that the
agency has improved its record of deporting "criminal aliens" and that

they are now 55 percent of the total deported vs. 35 percent at the beginning of the Obama administration. That group includes those who are flagged for deportation after being arrested for any potential violation, even misdemeanors.

19. Paul McEnroe, "U.S. Citizenship No Defense Against Deportation Threat," *Star Tribune*, November 27, 2011, http://www.startribune.com /local/north/134541773.html.

20. Dino Grandoni, "Obama Administration Nears Its Millionth Deportation," *Atlantic Wire*, September 9, 2011, http://www.theatlanticwire .com/national/2011/09/obama-administration-nears-its-millionth-depor tation/42302/.

21. ICE, Secure Communities Statistics, May 2011, http://www.ice.gov/doclib /foia/sc-stats/nationwide_interoperability_stats-fy2011-feb28.pdf.

22. Pilar Marrero, "Programa de ICE está bajo la lupa," *La Opinión*, November 24, 2011.

23. ICE, Secure Communities Website, http://www.ice.gov/secure_communi ties/.

24. Michael Hennessy, "Secure Communities Destroys Public Trust," *SFGate*, May 1, 2011, http://www.sfgate.com/cgi-bin/article.cgi?f=/c/a/2011/05/01 /INB81J8OCL.DTL.

25. Pilar Marrero, "Comunidades Seguras tiene más rechazo, Impre," *La Opinión*, June 2011.

26. Ibid.

27. Gretchen Gavett, "Why 3 Governors Challenged Secure Communities," *Frontline*, PBS, October 18, 2011, http://www.pbs.org/wgbh/pages/front line/race-multicultural/lost-in-detention/why-three-governors-challenged -secure-communities/.

28. Arturo Venegas, former police chief of Sacramento, California, interviewed by author, May 2011.

29. Pilar Marrero, "Deportación de criminales baja en vez de aumentar," *La Opinión*, May 17, 2012.

CHAPTER 14   THE REPUBLICANS

1. "Perry Fights Back on Immigration: 'You Don't Have a Heart,'" Republican primary debate, Fox Nation, September 22, 2011, http://nation .foxnews.com/rick-perry/2011/09/22/perry-fights-back-immigration-you -dont-have-heart.

2. Rachel Pugh, "Report Forecasts Educated Worker Shortage by 2018," Georgetown University, June 16, 2010, http://explore.georgetown.edu /news/?ID=51240.

3. Paul Steinhauser "Poll: 54 Percent Support DREAM Act," *Political Ticker*, December 10, 2010, http://politicalticker.blogs.cnn.com/2010/12/10/poll -54-percent-support-dream-act/.

4. Ioan Grillo, "Cain's Electrified-Border Joke: No Laughing Matter in Mexico," *Time*, October 17, 2011, http://www.time.com/time/world /article/0,8599,2097128,00.html#ixzz1xYd8zbh3.

5. Ed Pilkington, "Mitt Romney in Talks Over Nationwide Version of Tough State Immigration Laws," *Guardian* (UK), February 24, 2012, http://www .guardian.co.uk/world/2012/feb/24/kris-kobach-immigration-law-master mind.

6. David Edwards, Romney advocates 'self-deportation' for undocumented immigrants, The Raw Story, January 2012.

7. Paul Taylor, Mark Hugo Lopez, Jeffrey Passel, and Seth Motel, "Unauthorized Immigrants: Length of Residency, Patterns of Parenthood," Pew Research Center, December 1, 2011, http://www.pewhispanic .org/2011/12/01/unauthorized-immigrants-length-of-residency-patterns -of-parenthood/?src=prc-headline.

8. Pilar Marrero, "Newt Stuns in CNN Debate with a Call to Legalize Workers," *Huffington Post,* November 23, 2011, http://www.huffingtonpost .com/pilar-marrero/newt-stuns-in-cnn-debate-_b_1110661.html.

9. "Full Transcript: ABC News Iowa Republican Debate," ABC World News, December 11, 2011, http://abcnews.go.com/Politics/full-transcript-abc -news-iowa-republican-debate/story?id=15134849#.T-PC5cXNnNo.

10. Marshall Fitz, "Newt Gingrich's Twisted Take on Immigration Reform," Center for American Progress Action Fund, December 8, 2011, http:// www.americanprogressaction.org/issues/2011/12/gingrich_immigration .html.

11. Pilar Marrero, "Marco Rubio's Dream Act: Brought to You by the Same Folks Who Invented 'Self-Deportation,'" *Huffington Post,* April 11, 2012, http://www.huffingtonpost.com/pilar-marrero/marco-rubio-dream act -wit_b_1413132.html.

12. Republican presidential nominee Mitt Romney appeared in front of a Latino group (NALEO) in June 2012 and proposed a series of policy changes, including quick legal residence for STEM graduates and a quicker path to residency for immediate family of resident aliens, but rejected any idea for the legalization for the 11 million undocumented already in the country and supported the DREAM Act only for military service members.

CHAPTER 15   THE ECONOMY, IMMIGRANTS, AND THE FUTURE OF AMERICA

1. United States Department of Labor, "The U.S. Population Is Becoming Larger and More Diverse," http://www.dol.gov/oasam/programs/history /herman/reports/futurework/report/chapter1/main.htm.

2. Audrey Singer, Brookings Institute, interviewed by author, July 2011.

3. Travis Loller, "Many Immigrants Pay Up at Tax Time," Associated Press, April 11, 2008.

4. Elana Mater, "Immigration's Effect on Our Poorest Workers," *Sockeye* (Summer 2008): 38–41, http://www.willamette.edu/centers/publicpolicy /projects/oregonsfuture/PDFVol12no2/V12N2Mater-Pew.pdf.

5. "The Role of Immigrants in the U.S. Labor Market," The Congress of the United States—Congressional Budget Office, November 1, 2005, http:// www.cbo.gov/publication/17452; retrieved April 11, 2011.

6. Pilar Marrero, Pete Wilson news conference, *La Opinión,* November 1996.

7. Partnership for a New American Economy, "Not Coming to America: Why the US is Falling Behind in the Global Race for Talent," May 2012, http://www.renewoureconomy.org/not-coming.

8. Fareed Zakaria, "America Risks Losing Its Immigration Advantage," CNN, June 28, 2011, http://globalpublicsquare.blogs.cnn.com/2011/06/28 /america-risks-losing-its-immigration-advantage/.

9. Dowell Myers, USC demographer and urban planning professor, interviewed by author, April 2011.

10. Immigration Policy Center, "The Future of a Generation: How New Americans Will Help Support Baby Boomers," February14, 2012, http://www.immigrationpolicy.org/just-facts/future-generation-how-new-americans-will-help-support-retiring-baby-boomers.

11. Mitra Toossi, "Labor Force Projections to 2020::A More Slowly Growing Workforce," *Monthly Labor Review* vol. 135, no. 1 (January 2012): 43–64.

CHAPTER 16   IS THE AMERICAN DREAM DEAD?

1. Jeffrey M. Jones, "Americans' Views on Immigration Holding Steady," *Gallup Politics,* June 22, 2011, http://www.gallup.com/poll/148154/americans-views-immigration-holding-steady.aspx.

2. Roberto Suro and Marcelo Suárez Orozco, "From Ellis Island to an Electrified Fence, Why America Is So Torn on Immigration," *Washington Post,* October 21, 2011, http://www.washingtonpost.com/opinions/from-ellis-island-to-an-electrified-fence-immigration-myths-that-hold-us-back/2011/10/19/gIQAGrRC4L_story.html.

3. María Hinojosa, *Lost in Detention,* PBS, October 2011 http://www.pbs.org/wgbh/pages/frontline/lost-in-detention/.

4. Sandra Hernández, "A Lethal Limbo," *Los Angeles Times,* June 1, 2008, http://articles.latimes.com/2008/jun/01/opinion/op-hernandez1.

5. Miriam Jordan, "Immigration Audits Drive Illegal Workers Underground," *Wall Street Journal,* August 15, 2011, http://online.wsj.com/article/SB10001424053111904480904576496200011699920.html.

6. "Mitt Romney on Immigration: Say What?" Interview with *Lakeland Ledger* (Florida), May 25, 2007, YouTube, http://www.youtube.com/watch?v=_rr6-CcOJPw.

7. Hinojosa, *Lost in Detention.*

CHAPTER 17   DEMOGRAPHIC CHANGE WON'T WAIT

1. Joel Kotkin, "Joel Kotkin: Why America Will Still Lead the World in 2050," Reason TV, YouTube, June 2010, http://www.youtube.com/watch?v=zWHUsXQyLZs.

2. Ibid.

3. Ibid.

4. Pilar Marrero, "June Tracking Poll: Immigration Is a Critical Issue for Voters," *Latino Decisions,* June 9, 2011, http://www.latinodecisions.com/blog/2011/06/10/june-tracking-poll-immigration-is-a-critical-issue-for-voters/.

INDEX